SMALL SCREENS

SMALL SCREENS

Essays on Contemporary Australian Television

Edited by Michelle Arrow, Jeannine Baker and Clare Monagle

Monash University Publishing
Matheson Library and Information Services Building
40 Exhibition Walk
Monash University
Clayton, Victoria 3800, Australia
www.publishing.monash.edu

Monash University Publishing brings to the world publications which advance the best traditions of humane and enlightened thought.

Monash University Publishing titles pass through a rigorous process of independent peer review.

http://www.publishing.monash.edu/books/ss-9781925377101.html

Series: Cultural Studies

Design: Les Thomas

National Library of Australia Cataloguing-in-Publication entry:

Title:	Small screens : essays on contemporary Australian television / edited by Michelle Arrow, Jeannine Baker and Clare Monagle.
ISBN:	9781925377101 (paperback)
Subjects:	Television--Australia.
	Television--Australia--History
	Television programs--Australia.
	Television programs--Australia--History.
	Television programs--Australia--Anecdotes.
	Television programs--Australia--Public opinion
Other Creators/Contributors:	
	Arrow, Michelle, editor.
	Baker, Jeannine, editor.
	Monagle, Clare, editor.
Dewey number:	791.4570994

Printed in Australia by Griffin Press an Accredited ISO AS/NZS 14001:2004 Environmental Management System printer.

The paper this book is printed on is certified against the Forest Stewardship Council ® Standards. Griffin Press holds FSC chain of custody certification SGS-COC-005088. FSC promotes environmentally responsible, socially beneficial and economically viable management of the world's forests.

Contents

Introduction

MICHELLE ARROW, JEANNINE BAKER AND CLARE MONAGLE

Some Australians of a certain age love to describe what it was like when television arrived in 1956. They will tell you about watching the Melbourne Olympics at a neighbour's house, or in the shop window. For baby boomers, the new tube constituted a milestone up there with Kennedy's assassination and the dismissal. The television landscape has changed immeasurably since Bruce Gyngell declared "Welcome to Television". We can now watch when we want and where we want, on myriad devices. We are not stuck with Graham Kennedy and grainy black and white football replays. Television is free to air, live streaming, pay per view, subscriber channels, delivered to our pockets and laptops whenever we want it.

There is so much to watch. So much that it can sometimes feel like a form of cultural duty, keeping up with our small screens. There has been a proliferation of digital channels. We can catch up on missed programs easily via the web. The arrival of Netflix, Stan and Presto in 2015 has only added to our televisual obligations. Unless it is live sport or a reality show grand final, there is no longer any need for appointment viewing. Long gone are the days where families battled it out over *Young Talent Time* or the football at 6:30 on Saturday nights, or where we were forced to choose between *The Comedy Company* versus *60 Minutes*. We are now much more atomised in our viewing, able to pick and choose. In many cases, all members of a household can happily watch what they want, simultaneously. On public transport we used to lean over the shoulders of our fellow passengers to see what they are reading. Now we glimpse a flash of *Game of Thrones* or *Girls* on the number whatever bus.

What, then, of the national television culture? Among this diffusion, is Australian-ness still refracted on our screens? And do screens create our Australian-ness? In the heyday of Australian cultural nationalism in the 1970s and 1980s, a growing fascination with Australian history and the ready availability of investor finance saw a proliferation of television depictions of Australian identity and culture. Changing viewing habits, cuts to investment incentives and public funding of screen production, and almost two decades of culture wars on public broadcasting has changed Australia's television landscape. Streaming and sharing has transformed our viewing habits: will it change what we can watch? Does our television still tell Australian stories? Will it be able to do so into the future? ABC Managing Director Mark Scott warned in the Inaugural Brian Johns lecture that:

> There is such a hunger for Australian stories in all their guises, beyond reality and sport. However, finding local productions of drama, documentary and narrative comedy is a persistent challenge and one that has become even harder as a result of cuts over time in funding to the national broadcasters, *Screen Australia* and state-funded bodies.
>
> Why does all this matter?
>
> It matters because the work of the Australian content industry in telling Australian stories underpins Australian identity, culture and society.
>
> [...] Even in an increasingly fragmented world, Australian stories on television will continue to be shared. We need to look collaboratively and creatively at ways to ensure they are not sidelined, but remain a key feature of our media landscape.[1]

---

1   Mark Scott, 'The Future of the Australian Story', Inaugural Brian Johns Lecture, Macquarie University, 15 September 2015, http://about.abc.net.au/speeches/the-future-of-the-australian-story/.

Despite Scott's note of caution, *Small Screens* suggests that Australian television still retains a place at the centre of our national cultural life. Television commands enormous audiences compared to almost any other cultural form. The essays in this book show that television still makes a significant impact on our political, social and cultural life. Television programs make the news and reflect the news. Who could forget Kevin Rudd's toxic, wounded pride on *The Killing Season*? The unexpected ratings failure of Channel Nine's costly mini-series *Gallipoli*? The raw testimonies of women who escaped violent relationships in *Hitting Home*? The Abbott government's war on the ABC's *Q&A*? Gina Rinehart's legal action against *House of Hancock*? These were all television programs that burst the bounds of the small screen to take over headlines and (briefly) dominate the national conversation.

We asked our contributors to write about these programs, not as specialists in television studies, or as critics, but to consider them as windows onto national issues and conversations. As historians, we wanted to explore the place that television occupies in contemporary Australian life, and our contributors (many being historians themselves) accepted that challenge with enthusiasm. This is a book for anyone interested in contemporary Australian culture. It is intended to fill a 'middle space' between the immediacy of the daily news cycle of criticism and commentary, and the longer-term perspective of scholarly writing and analysis.

Small Screens consists of twelve essays on a range of noteworthy programs broadcast on Australian television in 2015. Our selection of programs is necessarily idiosyncratic: from *The Bachelor* to *The Killing Season*, *The Secret River* to *Struggle Street*, we have attempted to represent some of the scope and scale of drama, factual and serialised programs broadcast on television.

Nick Herd provides a roadmap to the transformations that have characterised the broadcasting industry in recent years: digital disruption, massive government funding cuts, and the arrival of overseas streaming services have changed the ways our television is made and consumed. In his chapter on *Making Australia Great* and *The Killing Season*, Mark Hearn reflects on the ways these programs reflected our political culture, which increasingly plays out as 'dismal soap opera'. Jeannine Baker examines the toll that successive funding changes have taken on our documentary production sector, astutely observing that changes to the commissioning and funding of one-off documentaries may jeopardise the broadcasting of distinctively Australian stories.

One of the big surprises of 2015 was the resounding failure of Anzac-themed television series. While record crowds turned out to dawn services and Anzac marches across the country, they didn't watch Channel 9's big-budget miniseries *Gallipoli*. Carolyn Holbrook argues that this series (and all Anzac-themed dramas) failed because it has proved impossible to dislodge Peter Weir's film *Gallipoli* from its central position in the national memory of Anzac.

Sarah Pinto compares the rapturous reception for the ABC adaptation of Kate Grenville's novel *The Secret River* with the critical local response to the BBC series *Banished*, which featured no Indigenous characters. Defamation law specialist David Rolph surveys the fascinating legal travails of *House of Hancock*, pointing out the risks that docudrama producers face in dramatising the lives of living people, particularly litigious ones like Gina Rinehart. Liz Giuffre considers the use of music in the latest dramatisation of the life of songwriter and performer Peter Allen, *Not the Boy Next Door*, and argues that the miniseries' use of music television nostalgia foregrounds the importance of television in Allen's rise to fame.

David Nichols celebrates thirty years of *Neighbours* with an affectionate, but critical, appraisal of the show set in Australia's most recognisable cul-de-sac. Jodi McAlister, herself a Bachie blogger, situates the dating show phenomenon in the long and changing history of romance narratives. Zora Simic investigates *Struggle Street*, assessing its claims to offer genuine class analysis, against the accusations of poverty porn. She reads *Struggle Street* amidst other depictions of Westies. Michelle Arrow suggests that the ABC programs *Judith Lucy is All Woman* and *Hitting Home* marked a year of feminist television, amplifying public conversations about gender inequality in Australia. In 'A bitter pill to swallow' Clare Monagle analyses the work done by food on our screens, arguing that food is never just fuel, but constitutes an imaginary of both nationhood and purity.

Taken together, our sample of programs reveals Australian television as a place that revels in bourgeois aspiration. Our screens insist that we try to eat clean, fall in love and keep a modern home. At the same time, cautionary tales are rolled out every night, to remind the viewer of what will happen if they fail to join this middle-class ideal. Images of the under-class and the overweight are often deployed to signify rejection from this wholesome national fantasy. And this wholesome national fantasy, when these accounts of major Australian television programs are read as a group, reveals a whiteness at its core. While a number of our contributors addressed race within their essays, and bearing in mind the presence of such programs as *Black Comedy* and, in the years preceding 2015 (which has been the focus of this book), *Redfern Now*, *Legally Brown*, and *The Gods of Wheat Street*, it is salutary to consider Australian screens collectively and register the general whiteness of both the shows' creators and their on-screen talent. There have been more laudable attempts over the past twelve months to shed light on important social issues, most particularly on *Prison Songs* and *Hitting Home*, which have incorporated race sensitively into their analysis. But these are the exceptions that prove the rule, alas. Television may have changed greatly since 1956, but it seems that a dominant imagined whiteness remains the same.

Television, then, does a lot of work culturally, for better or for worse. Join our contributors as they delineate, appreciate, ponder and take to task the stuff that we watch on the tube in Australia.

CHAPTER 1

The Televisual Landscape Today

NICK HERD

We may have plenty to read and watch as audience members, but is it the kind of content that makes us informed citizens; that reveals what some people want concealed; that holds the powerful to account? That helps Australians understand each other better and the world in which we live? Where is the content that leaves us as not just sated audiences and primed consumers, but informed citizens?

Mark Scott,[1] Managing Director, Australian Broadcasting Corporation

Introduction

Reports of the early death of free to air television are premature. A lot of attention has been paid to the changing digital landscape in television, particularly the arrival of Netflix to Australia early in 2015, and to what that might mean for the so-called 'legacy' television service providers, such as the national and commercial broadcasters. The impression one could get from some of this hype is that broadcast television has changed forever and that it is possibly on the way out, as these new forms of television enter the market and audiences are presented with new ways to access television programming. However,

---

1   Mark Scott, 'The Future of the Australian Story', Inaugural Brian Johns Lecture, Macquarie University, 15 September 2015, http://about.abc.net.au/speeches/the-future-of-the-australian-story/.

there is a danger that we are overestimating the short run impact of this disruption and underestimating the longer impacts of change.

While it is true that in 2015 the number of people watching free to air television did decline, there are still a lot of people watching broadcast television; the old fashioned 'linear television'. This is demonstrated by the *Australian Multi Screen Report*, published every quarter by Oztam and Nielsen. In Quarter 2 of 2015, on average, Australians watched 90:53 hours of broadcast television per month, of which 8:11 hours was played back on a television set. They also watched 7:32 hours of video on a PC/laptop, 2:47 hours on a smartphone and 2:03 hours on a tablet. Not surprisingly teens watched the least amount of broadcast television and those over 60 the most. People aged 18–24 watched the most video on devices other than a television (26:41 hours per month).[2] In 2015 the top ten programs on free to air television attracted an average of more than two million viewers.

These are not figures that suggest the imminent death of broadcast television. This is not to say there has been no change and the sector does not face some challenges, not least from new entrants to the market, which it is trying to address or will have to address. In this chapter I will be looking at some of these challenges and some of the significant events during 2015, with reference to free to air television and subscription television, including cable, satellite and IPTV, from the point of view of the changes to the business or the regulatory environment.

But first, a brief bit of context. In relation to free to air television Australia still maintains the dual system of national and commercial television that has been in place since television started in 1956. The national broadcasters – the ABC and the SBS – are statutory

2   Oztam, Regional TAM & Nielsen, 2015, *Australian Multiscreen Report: Quarter 2 2015*, www.oztam.com.au/documents/Other/Australian%20Multi%20Screen%20 Report%20Q2%202015%20FINAL.pdf, p.7.

corporations, which receive direct funding from the Australian Government, but also earn revenue by other means, such as program sales and merchandising or in the case of the SBS from advertising. The commercial broadcasters are licensed under the *Broadcasting Services Act* ('the Act') to provide metropolitan and regional services and are supported by advertising. They are subject to various regulatory requirements including those relating to minimum levels of Australian content. Subscription television, delivered by cable and satellite, is also licensed under the Act and supported by revenue from subscribers and the sale of advertising time. Cable and satellite television providers are subject to lesser regulatory requirements, but still need to deliver minimum amounts of Australian drama content. IPTV, including services such as Netflix, Stan and YouTube are not regulated by the Act and do not need any government oversight to operate. Table 1 sets out the main television providers in Australia.

Table 1 – Main Television Providers in Australia – November 2015

	FTA-Metro	FTA-Regional	STV/SVOD
National	ABC	ABC	
National	SBS	SBS	
Commercial	Seven West Media	Prime	
Commercial	Nine Entertainment	Southern Cross	
Commercial	Ten Holdings	WIN Television	
STV			Foxtel
SVOD			Netflix
SVOD			Stan

Change is Constant

Over the past two decades there has been the complete switch off of analogue television and the transition to digital terrestrial television for the free to air broadcasters. The transition took over a decade from 2001 up to the end of 2013. The transition was initiated and managed by the government so as to have the least amount of disruption to the existing business models of terrestrial broadcasters. This transition brought with it the introduction of free to air multi-channelling, and the launch of the Freeview brand in 2008, as the main incentive to convince Australian consumers to invest in the digital transition. The commercial and national broadcasters now provide at least two and, in some cases, three additional free television channels, all available on the same terrestrial platform. The result is that there is more free television available than ever before.

Television you pay for has been with us since the introduction of the VCR around 1980, but subscription television broadcasting commenced in Australia in 1995, utilising a mix of satellite, micro-wave and cable as delivery platforms; and with a number of competing providers, including Foxtel, Austar and Optus. Since that time competition has been rationalised so that today Foxtel is the sole provider of subscription television. The penetration of subscription television has been stuck around 30% for some years, but PwC predicts it will continue to rise (to around 37% by 2019).[3]

Catch up television started in 2008 when the ABC started its iView service, which is delivered over the internet and can be watched on a television set, a tablet or any mobile device. The other free to air broadcasters all now provide some form of catch up service free to viewers.

More recently there has been the introduction of Subscription Video on Demand (SVOD) services, of which more below.

3   Price Waterhouse Coopers, *Australian Media and Entertainment Outlook 2015–19*, Sydney, 2015.

Commercial Television

The Seven Network ended the ratings year at number one for the ninth year in a row. The Nine Network won in the key advertising demographic of 18–49 year olds. TEN also saw its ratings increase after some bad years. However, despite this good news for the commercial sector, the number of people watching the three commercial networks in prime time (6–12pm) declined by 11.2% over the year.[4] The results are set out in Table 2 below.

Table 2 – Prime Time Ratings (6pm–12midnight) – Live and Catch Up, Including All Channels[5]

	Total % share	16–39 % share	18–49 % share	25–54 % share
ABC	17.6	10.5	11.4	12.1
Seven	29.3	28	28.1	28.3
Nine	28.1	30.8	30.3	30.2
TEN	18.8	25.5	24.7	23.7
SBS	6.2	5.1	5.5	5.7

The reasons for this decline are not simple. For those that believe in the impact of digital disruption the cause is seen as the new SVOD services, like Netflix, that are presenting consumers with more choice. Peter Ryan of Carat media said of the audience: "They are now finding bespoke media content for themselves and not just

4   N. Christensen, 'Were there any real winners in the last TV ratings year?', *Mumbrella*, 2015, http://mumbrella.com.au/were-there-any-real-winners-in-the-last-tv-ratings-year-333035?utm_medium=email&utm_campaign=Mumbrella%20daily%20newsletter%20December%202%20 2015&utm_content=Mumbrella%20daily%20newsletter%20December%202%20 2015+CID_f4166dd417c36060141c11c0067e3491&utm_source=Campaign%20 Monitor&utm_term=Continue%20Reading.

5   Don Groves, 'Strong year for Australian TV drama', *IF Magazine*, http://if.com. au/2015/11/29/article/Strong-year-for-Australian-TV-drama/KPYSCKFBJZ.html 30/11/2015 and Seven West Media http://www.sevenwestmedia.com.au/docs/default-source/business-unit-news/2015-survey-release.pdf?sfvrsn=4, 30 November 2015.

accepting what is on TV. They are chasing their own content to suit their own needs and their own interests".[6] On the other hand the networks made mistakes with programming during the year, such as putting programs of similar genres up against each other in the same timeslots e.g. *Reno Rumble* against *House Rules*. It certainly is the case that that innovation in programming was not a strong suit in 2015 and some formats have been around for some time. All the prime time reality formats, except for *MasterChef* and *The Bachelor*, lost audience share during the year.[7]

In terms of what was most watched in 2015, as in other years, sport and reality style programming dominate the list shown in Table 3. This indicates the extent to which commercial television differentiates itself through live programming that cannot be sourced through any other platform. The strength of free to air television will continue to be the provision of live events which are mostly sport.

Table 3 – Top 10 Single Programs[8]

Top 10 Single Programs: All people five, capitals, live and catch up
AFL Grand Final
State of Origin Rugby League – second match
Rugby League Grand Final
ICC Cricket World Cup – Final Session
State of Origin Rugby League– Match 1
State of Origin Rugby League– Match 3
AFL Grand Final – Presentations
MasterChef – Winner Announced
My Kitchen Rules - Winner Announced
My Kitchen Rules – Final

6   Christensen, op cit.

7   P. Kalina, 2015, 'Networks can all cheer in TV ratings war', *Sun-Herald*, 29 November, p.30.

8   P. Kalina, 'SBS and Ten are the winners in a sea of red ink', *The Guide, Sydney Morning Herald*, 7 December 2015, p.5.

The importance of live sport for commercial television was dramatically illustrated in August when the AFL signed a new deal with existing broadcasters Seven, Foxtel and Telstra for the period 2017 to 2022 worth $2.5 billion. Previously the partners had been paying $250 million a year for these rights, but in future will be paying $418 million.[9] It was not revealed how much of that will be paid for by Seven, but they face escalating costs in a future where revenue will not be growing.

PwC in their annual *Australian Entertainment and Media Outlook* predict that in the five years to 2019 the advertising revenue for commercial television will stagnate, with little or no growth. In 2014 commercial television advertising revenue was worth $3.8 billion. In comparison internet advertising revenue amounted to $4.4 billion in 2014 and is predicted by PwC to grow to $8.2 billion by 2019. Put another way, the prospect for commercial television is that over the next five years the total advertising market in Australia will grow healthily, but the share attributed to commercial television will decline.[10]

Measurement has been a problem as new devices and platforms spring up for watching television. Audience measurement is crucial to the business of advertiser supported television since it is on the basis of reported viewers that advertising time is sold. Oztam, the company owned by the broadcasters, which undertakes the ratings research, has at the time of writing been working on a new measurement service that will track viewing across all the platforms and which it hopes to launch in late 2015 or early 2016.

---

9   Australian Football League, 'AFL signs new six-year, $2.5 billion broadcast rights deal', 18 August 2015, www.afl.com.au/news/2015-08-18/afl-on-the-verge-of-signing-new-tv-deal.

10   PwC, op cit.

Ownership Rule Changes

The biggest change to the ownership of Australian media occurred in the late 80s as a result of changes to media ownership law in 1986 which prevented cross media ownership and abolished the two station rule in favour of the audience reach rule. At the same time the policy of equalisation through aggregation of regional licence areas meant that the majority of the population had access to three commercial television services. The immediate impact was that the power of the Sydney and Melbourne stations was reinforced as they became the centre of national networks and gained power over regional television programming and access to some of their revenue streams. Aggregation was initially an economic disaster for regional television, which took at least five years to adjust and required the government to grant rebates on licence fees to assist with the transition.

By the end of 2015 the Government had all but decided that the ownership laws needed to be changed because they were outdated. The four regional television broadcasters – Prime, WIN, Southern Cross and Imparja – had put the case that they no longer made sense when there was so much competition from internet delivered services, including, most importantly, the catch up services of free-to-air competitors, perhaps the biggest threats to the advertising revenue and financial base of these regional broadcasters. They argued that the ownership laws restricted them from growing and achieving economies of scale, so that with rising cost pressures their ability to provide local programming would likely be affected. They launched a public campaign, fronted by ex-Deputy Prime Minister Tim Fischer, called *Save our Voices*, which highlighted the threat to regional news and current affairs. Legislative change will likely happen in 2016 and result in a round of mergers and acquisitions.

The National Broadcasters

The ABC and the SBS of course provide both television and radio services. The SBS operates one national radio network and the ABC six. Both operate four television channels and a catch up service. In addition the SBS is a partner in two subscription television channels. While the ABC broadcasts in only English the SBS provides programming in 74 languages. The ABC has 12 international news bureaux and is also in the retail business with ABC Shops around the country. Table 4 provides a snapshot comparison of the relative size of the two national broadcasters.

The ABC has also developed an extensive online presence and has been a pioneer amongst all broadcasters in utilising online as a means of extending its national presence and increasing access to its programming. The success of this strategy has caused some concern to commercial rivals, who see the ABC as a competitor.

Table 4 – Comparison Between the ABC and SBS[11]

	ABC	SBS
Cost of Services	$1215m	$377.5m
Own Revenue	$175.5m	$103.9m
Government Funding	$1244.6m	$351.7m
Staff	4,580	1084
Australian content TV	64%	39%
Average weekly TV reach	14 million people	7 million people

Cuts to the ABC budget

Going into the 2013 election the Abbott government promised that there would be no cuts to the ABC or to the SBS if they were elected. However, following the election then Minister for Communications,

---

11 Department of Communications, 2014, ABC and SBS Efficiency Study, Draft Report, www.communications.gov.au/sites/g/files/net301/f/ABC_and_SBS_efficiency_report_Redacted.pdf.

Malcolm Turnbull, announced that his department, with the assistance of Peter Lewis, ex-CFO of Seven West Media, would undertake an efficiency review of both national broadcasters. The review was completed before the 2014 Budget, but not released until later in the year.

In that budget the announcement was made that the ABC and SBS would get an immediate budget cut of 1% as a "down payment" on further cuts to be identified in the efficiency review. At the time it was reported that Minister Turnbull had resisted larger cuts, including the imposition of an efficiency dividend of the kind that applies to other government agencies.[12]

The Government also cancelled the contract the ABC had with the Department of Foreign Affairs and Trade to deliver the Australia Network, the Asia-Pacific television service, which was worth $220 million over ten years to the ABC. This cancellation was not unexpected, as the Government had been highly critical in opposition of the way the Gillard government had handled the awarding of the contract to the ABC over private interests bidding for it.

When the efficiency review was released in November 2014 it identified the following areas where efficiencies could be achieved:

- Greater operational co-operation between the ABC and SBS
- Use of new technologies
- Better integration of the national broadcasters with the wider broadcasting and production sectors
- Earning additional revenue
- Better resource allocation

---

12 L. Metherill, 'Budget 2014: ABC, SBS funding cut, Australia Network contract cancelled', ABC Online, www.abc.net.au/news/2014-05-13/budget-2014-abc,-sbs-funding-cut,-ausnet-contract-cancelled/5450932.

In November 2014 Minister Turnbull announced the outcome of the review would be a cut to the ABC budget of $254 million over five years, or 4.6% of the total budget. The SBS would receive a cut of $25.2 million or 1.7% over the same period.

In making the announcement of the cuts Minister Turnbull warned the ABC:

> There is a temptation for management to blame the Government for some of these program changes. That would be cowardly. The ABC management know that they can meet these savings without reducing the resources available to programming – furthermore they know that the Government and their board know too.[13]

The response of the ABC was announced by ABC Managing Director Mark Scott and included closing the Adelaide television production studio and winding back remaining production activities in the smaller states, closing five regional radio posts, ceasing state-based local sports coverage and rationalising the use of television outside broadcast vans. Four hundred staff, or 10% of the workforce, would be made redundant. Programming changes in television included moving to a national end of week version of *The 7.30 Report* and shifting *Lateline* to News 24 from 2016.

In a move probably unrelated to the Budget cuts in July 2015 the ABC announced that there would be a phased closure of its ABC retail shops as the corporation moved to an entirely online retail strategy.

---

13 ABC Online, 'ABC funding to be cut by $254 million over five years, Communications Minister Malcolm Turnbull says', www.abc.net.au/news/2014-11-19/abc-funding-cuts-announced-by-malcolm-turnbull/5902774, 20 November 2014.

SBS Advertising

SBS Television is allowed to broadcast 120 minutes of advertising in a day and no more than 5 minutes in any one hour. In comparison commercial television broadcasters may screen over 300 minutes of advertising and non-program matter in a day and up to 13 minutes an hour in prime time. To offset some of the cuts the Government had planned to raise $28 million in additional revenue for SBS by increasing the limit on advertising to 10 minutes in the hour. This required a legislative amendment to the *SBS Act*, but in June 2015 the ALP and the Greens combined in the Senate to defeat the legislation. The SBS said at the time that it had exhausted all efficiency measures and that "… this funding cut is unable to be absorbed without impacting programs and services".[14] Free TV, the association representing commercial television, saw the defeat as a positive move for their sector.

The Q&A Incident

The editorial independence of the ABC came under serious scrutiny in June 2015 and faced heated criticism from elements of the Abbott Government. Zaky Mallah, who had been tried and acquitted of terrorism charges in 2005, was part of the audience for *Q&A* and participated in an exchange with the Parliamentary Secretary to the Foreign Affairs Minister, Steven Ciobo. Parts of Mallah's remarks were interpreted as being an incitement to join ISIS. Prime Minister Abbott reacted angrily to the incident, asking the ABC "whose side are you on?"

ABC Managing Director, Mark Scott, responded: "At times, free speech principles mean giving platforms to those with whom

---

14 Mumbrella, 'Senate defeats proposed legislation to allow SBS to double advertising in prime time', http://mumbrella.com.au/senate-defeats-proposed-legislation-to-allow-sbs-to-double-advertising-in-prime-time-301676, 24 June 2015.

we fundamentally disagree ..."[15] However, the ABC did apologise for the incident and transfer the program from the current affairs division to the news division. Late in 2015 an independent survey of the program chaired by former Managing Director of SBS Shaun Brown and journalist Ray Martin reported no evidence of left bias.

Subscription Television

Foxtel

Foxtel continues to be a joint venture between Telstra Corporation and 20th Century Fox, a News Ltd company. It is delivered by cable and satellite, has been completely digital since 2007 and has the potential to reach about 70% of television households. The platform carries nearly 300 channels; including HD versions of channels, time delayed movies and the rebroadcast of free to air channels. Subscribers are offered channels in bundles, access to a personal video recorder (Foxtel IQ), on demand movies and television, pay per view events and an SVOD service, Presto. Some of the channels are owned and operated by Foxtel, but most are packaged for the platform by other providers.

In early 2015 Foxtel rolled out its new 'triple play' bundle, in which it offers internet, phone and subscription television in one bundle. Shortly after, it dropped its entry level price to $25 a month; by adding sport, which is the service's most watched product, the cost rises to $50 a month. In early December 2015 Foxtel reported that it had recorded an 8.6% increase in subscribers for the year, to around 2,850,000 subscribers, but this included an unspecified number of

---

15 Matthew Knott, 'Q&A: Mark Scott fires back at Tony Abbott, saying ABC is not "a state broadcaster"', *Sydney Morning Herald*, 26 June 2015, www.smh.com. au/federal-politics/political-news/qa-mark-scott-fires-back-at-tony-abbott-saying-abc-is-not-a-state-broadcaster-20150625-ghxr9g.html#ixzz3tbkS1zXN.

subscribers to Presto. Revenue also increased for the 2015 financial year by just under 2%, to $3.15 billion.[16]

The increase in subscribers will likely make advertising a more important part of the revenue mix for Foxtel. Multi-Channel Network, which is a joint venture between Foxtel and Fox Sports, has since 2014 offered advertisers access to consumers based on their actual purchasing behavior rather than standard demographics. However, the biggest inhibitors to subscriber growth are the lack of exclusive access to live sport and the high cost of the service, compared to subscription television in the USA and UK. The profitability of Foxtel is actually built on the willingness of many subscribers to pay as much as $100 a month for the service.

In June 2015 Foxtel announced that it was acquiring 15% of the shares in Ten Network Holdings, owner of the TEN Network, worth about $77 million. At the same time Ten Network Holdings acquired a 25% share of Multi-Channel Network, which took over all advertising sales for TEN.

SVOD

The SVOD providers in Australia as of November 2015 are Apple TV, T-Box (Telstra), Fetch TV, Presto, Stan, Quickflix and Netflix. A study by research company Edentify showed an increase in the number of Australians watching IPTV. For the purposes of the study IPTV includes the broadcast networks catch up services, SVOD and free services like YouTube. Published in November it showed that 48% of Australians had watched television programming or film online in the previous month and that the audience is growing, with

---

16 Mumbrella, 'Foxtel admits subscriber figures include Presto users but claims cable still biggest growth driver', 8 December 2015, http://mumbrella.com.au/foxtel-admits-subscriber-figures-include-presto-users-but-claims-cable-still-biggest-growth-driver-311968.

the figure being higher, at 59%, for people under 50.[17] The most popular services were YouTube and the catch up services, but there was also strong growth for Netflix.

Much has been made of the disruptive impact of these new services on broadcast television and its traditional business model.[18] But the business that has really been disrupted by SVOD is retail sales of DVDs and the DVD rental market. These markets have declined from revenue of $1.6 billion in 2010 to just on $1 billion, with the rental market being particularly hard hit. PwC predicts continuing shrinkage of revenues through to 2019.

ABC Managing Director Mark Scott was among those who suggested SVOD services be required to spend a certain amount of their revenue on local content. There is presently no Australian content regulation for these kinds of services, as there is for commercial and subscription television. Subscription television has been required to spend a percentage of their program expenditure on drama channels on new Australian drama.

Assuming there was the political will to achieve such an outcome the Australian Government ceded some of its flexibility to act in relation to these kinds of services when it entered into the Australia US Free Trade Agreement over a decade ago. Whereas the US was perfectly amenable to grandfathering existing content regulation on commercial and subscription television, as long as it was never increased, they were not happy about assuming future services would be subject to similar regulation.

The Agreement states that if the Australian Government finds that Australian content on such channels is 'not readily available to Australian consumers' it can act to ensure that 'access to such

---

17 'More Aussies watching IPTV', B&T, http://www.bandt.com.au/media/aussies-watching-iptv.

18 See for example Michael Mullins, 'Netflix and Fairfax in an uncaring new media environment', *Eureka Street*, Vol. 25, No. 6, 2015, pp.36–37.

programming on interactive audio and/or video services is not unreasonably denied to Australian consumers'. Such regulation must not be burdensome, more trade restrictive than is necessary or applied to a business operating outside of Australia. Consultation with affected parties, which would include the service providers and most likely also the US government, would also be required.

Television Production

The Australian independent screen production sector relies heavily upon television for the viability of the sector. At the 2015 Screen Producers Conference in November, veteran producer John Edwards (*Love Child, Love My Way, The Secret Life of Us*) delivered the Hector Crawford memorial lecture, in which he lamented the state of Australian television drama production. He saw it as characterised by fewer series, the same writers and directors, increased costs with no increase in quality, and declining audiences: "All the openness and excitement and bringing through of new talent, of new work, has certainly dissipated, and the area that has historically been the largest and most productive sector (long form series drama) of the broadcast industry has all but disappeared".[19]

As Table 5 indicates Australian television drama expenditure decreased in 2014–15 by 13% while the number of hours broadcast decreased by 14%. In the ten years to 2014–15 the number of hours of drama broadcast has decreased by 17%, while the total spending increased by 32%. As Edwards indicated that is more money being spent for fewer hours of drama, which is of increasing concern to the production sector.

---

19 D. Groves, 'Edwards laments lack of new drama and talent', *If Magazine*,
    http://if.com.au/2015/11/17/article/Edwards-laments-lack-of-new-dramas-and-
    talent/SLHLABONBA.html.

Table 5 – Australian Television Drama Production[20]

	#Titles	Hours	Spend $m
2010/11	41	583	337
2011/12	45	549	293
2012/13	57	661	374
2013/14	51	603	343
2014/15	47	517	299

However, if this poses an issue for the creative and financial viability of the independent production sector, it is not being reflected in what people watch. In 2015 the most popular drama programs on television were telemovies, miniseries or short run series, as indicated by Table 6. For the most part they were Australian, with very few foreign dramas attracting large audiences.

Table 6 – Top 10 Drama Programs[21]

Top 10 Drama Programs
All people, five capitals, live and catch up
House of Hancock
Peter Allen: Not the Boy Next Door
Gallipoli – Launch
800 Words
The Doctor Blake Mysteries
The Big Bang Theory (US)
New Tricks (UK)
Love Child
Winter
Foyle's War (UK)

20 Screen Australia, Drama report: Production of feature films and TV drama in Australia 2014–15.
21 P. Kalina, 'SBS and Ten are the winners in a sea of red ink', *The Guide, Sydney Morning Herald*, 7 December 2015, p.5.

Thirty years ago Australia launched the first of its domestic communications satellites. It was the dawn of the current revolution in information and communications technologies, but the best use that could be found for the satellite was basic telephony and broadcast television. The result was the facilitation of national networking, which truly bound Australia in both space and time and handed to the television networks significantly increased control over content production.

That power is being undermined by the rise of the internet as a service platform and as a new means of distributing and creating content. As argued above, this does not mean the death of broadcast television. In Australia the audiovisual production sector is still very dependent upon broadcast television, but that will have to change. The biggest challenge facing the production sector is how to absorb the internet into production and business strategies. This is more than having a strategy for a web presence; it means understanding how the web can extend both productivity and revenue. The YouTube generation are the future consumers of audiovisual.

CHAPTER 2

A Bitter Pill to Swallow

Food on Australian TV

CLARE MONAGLE

Michelle Bridges, one of the frightening trainers on *The Biggest Loser*, announced her pregnancy to *Who* magazine in July 2015 and explained her late-in-life fecundity as a result of her high health standards. Standing next to her in a series of photos was Commando, her equally intimidating *Biggest Loser* colleague, as well as her life partner and the father of her unborn child. In the glossy spread, Michelle explained how she had been able to beat the odds and become pregnant naturally at the historically geriatric age (in pregnancy terms) of 44. Michelle said:

> All of my years and all of Steve's years of looking after ourselves and taking care of our health and our bodies – it just goes to show for someone my age for it to happen so quickly it's obviously got to do with good health.[1]

A number of fertility experts, prevailed upon by the blogosphere, chimed in with strong responses to Bridges' claims. Their consensus was that Bridges' aged pregnancy ought to be understood as the result of luck. The odds are against a woman in mid-life conceiving, but it is not impossible. That is how odds work. Lady fortune smiled on Mich and Commando, and now Australia will be blessed by the merging of their gene pools.

Bridges' comments reveal a disturbing contemporary fantasy visible across Australian screens. This is the idea that we are what we eat,

---

1   'We're having a baby', *Who*, July 27, 2015.

but not only physically. We are what we eat spiritually, emotionally and morally. Good things come to those who 'look after themselves', who practice self-care. The more pure goodness we put into our bodies, the more good things will come our way. That is the essential take home from Bridges' comments; the idea that we can control ourselves, and our world, through the management of our bodies.

This is also the unspoken idea that is being preached by wellness advocates such as Sarah Wilson, Paleo Pete Evans and Smoothie Sally Obermeder. Tanned, lean and lissom, they have all built on television profiles to become gurus of goodness. They are the poster-people for their organic revolutions from within. Sort out your gut flora, and the rest will follow. Eschew 'chemicals', eat 'clean', go 'paleo', and you too might glow as if you are surrounded by sensitive lighting and a hair and make-up team. Your Breton striped shirt will pulsate with your energies, and your artfully tied top-knot will radiate the sun-kissed highlights you received while paddle-boarding. No bogan soft drinks for you, no tim tams, no junk food. Just tuck into some 'natural' foods, such as 'ancient' grains and beef just as the cavemen enjoyed it.

There was a time, apparently, before industrialisation, where things were idyllic. When we all exchanged our goods through bartering, at farmers markets. This was a time when there was no obesity and no diabetes.

A related, pervasive food fantasy dancing across Australian television, is that you are what you cook. Masterchef has taught us this. 'Put yourself on the plate' and 'Cook from the heart'. Among the exposed brick of Masterchef's *mise-en-place*, George, Gary and Matt exhort the contestants to look within themselves and find their essential self. They then ask them to pour that selfhood on the plate into a creation that embodies their ethnicity, as well as their love for family and their imbrication in community. Then, George, Gary and Matt eat this selfhood, look quizzical, and tell the contestant what is wrong with their dish. You have put yourself on the plate, and we are here to tell you that you are too salty, undercooked and, frankly, not to our taste. There will be flames, there will be Katy Perry, and back Amina or Alvin go to the bosom of home.

Food does a lot of work on Australian television, as it does more broadly in our culture. We display our taste through the tastes that we indulge. In Australia we are swamped with caloric possibility. In our suburbs we drive past multiple fast food outlets on every trip, each promising glistening affordable salty joy. In our gentrified inner cities, we walk or bike past the organic cafes and health-food stores that are proliferating. At the former we are served by uniformed employees, drilled in the art of upselling extra fries. At the latter we are served by employees in a different type of uniform, that of the large leather apron, ironic 501s and a bushy beard. In both cases, however, they sell relatively affordable abundance, geared to your class and geographical position. How we eat, and where we buy it, marks us out in all sorts of ways. Food is never just fuel, it is a measure of how we interact with the world around us, in the most literal and carnal of ways. And this plays out to the max in visual screen cultures, where our worthiness can be so easily signified through our visages. Contestants on the Biggest Loser are edited so that misery and shame seem to be written on their bodies, rendering them as fat bogans in need of a makeover stat. Matt Preston's girth, on the other hand, is cravatted in fabulous fabrics, and is a measure of his exuberant but gourmet carnality. His fat is fine, because it doesn't come with a side of underclass despair.

In what follows, I will discuss two recent moments when our screen food fantasies became unstuck. The unmasking of the fraudulent wellness blogger Belle Gibson revealed the credulity with which we consume stories of wellbeing through food. In this case, a number of media outlets had reported that the telegenic Belle had cured her cancer by eating organic. When it became apparent that she had lied about having cancer, she was excoriated in the press. As swiftly as this young woman had been elevated, she was then punished. In particular, her humiliation came at the hands of *60 Minutes*, a program that has never feared taking the high middle ground. And Annabel Crabb's interview with Scott Morrison as part of her *Kitchen Cabinet* program was also the subject of some controversy. Many viewers were pained and angered by the easy ride they felt that Crabb gave Morrison, suggesting that the light-hearted tone of the program let him off the hook all too easily for his policies. The argument of Crabb's program is that cooking and eating reveals the more human side of politicians. Many of Crabb's critics, however, felt that Morrison did not warrant this humanisation, given the inhumane nature of his policies. He may have revealed his love of Sri Lankan cuisine on Crabb's program, but his political actions revealed his overall contempt for those seeking asylum from that same region. *Kitchen Cabinet*, on which there has only been two non-white guests, reveals the shallowness of our multicultural engagement. We might eat food from all over the world, but our politicians represent a very particular type of Australia. The cases of Gibson and Morrison both reveal our cultural desire to invest in the meanings of food, and the credulity we risk when we do so.

Entrée

Our hunger to assign deep significance to consumption can be seen very sharply in the case study of Gibson, wellness entrepreneur turned publically-shamed fraud. Gibson came to public attention in 2013 when she announced that she had managed her brain cancer through organic foods and natural therapies. Gibson was, and I suppose must still be, a radiantly beautiful, apple-cheeked, young woman. She has long blonde hair and shiny scrubbed skin. She looks very well indeed. She was a mother of one, an infant son, a fact that added piquancy to her plucky story of self-devised recovery. Gibson built a big brand very fast. She deployed social media expertly in order to image her blonde vitality into a health promise. Eating clean, for Gibson, meant that she had scrubbed the cancer out of her insides and was pure again. Gibson was the cherubic child of new media, able to exploit the credulity of her Instagram followers to insist that she offered a proven way to health. She parlayed it all into her very successful app *The Whole Pantry*. And wait, there's more, she promised that proceeds would go to charity.

Old media took notice of Belle's success. She appeared on Sunrise in 2014 with Samantha Armytage and Andrew O'Keefe gushing over her remarkable recovery, and telling her how well she looked.[2] Gibson was shown meditating in her minimalist white-interiored townhouse, as well as cuddling her toddler tow-headed son. She was described as an 'ecopreneur'. Armytage and O'Keefe were dazzled, 'Belle, you're fabulous' gushed Armytage, 'for a person living with brain cancer, might I add, you look incredibly healthy'. Armytage declared *The Whole Pantry* 'a sexy app' (unfortunately reprising hideous memories of her brief show *Bringing Sexy Back*). Gibson was awarded one of Cosmopolitan Magazine's *Fun Fearless Female* awards. She accepted her award, dressed in white, and declared:

> At the end of the day I'm just human and I'm incredibly
> honoured that people do want to share my life and I want to
> share yours as well. I'm really honoured that we can come
> together on a platform like Instagram, Facebook, Twitter and
> share those moments together.[3]

2   'Health, Wellness and Lifestyle App', *Sunrise*, broadcast 28 February 2014 https://au.tv.yahoo.com/sunrise/video/watch/21742703/health-wellness-and-lifestyle-app/#page1.

3   'Belle Gibson Healer: She definitely had Cancer', *Cosmopolitan*, www.cosmopolitan.com.au/health-lifestyle/lifestyle/2015/4/belle-gibson-interview-aww/.

Gibson had built her empire on a dextrous use of many platforms, prioritising image over evidence, and she got away with it for some time. She was lauded in myriad publications, facts went unchecked, and she made a lot of money. The faith that met her extraordinary claims of fruit and vegetable based healing testifies to the desire of many to believe that organic miracles do happen, even without a whit of proof.

It did not last, however. Fairfax reported in early 2015 that a number of charities to which Gibson said she had donated money had not received any cash.[4] *The Australian* followed up Gibson's cancer claims, ascertaining that there was no evidence whatsoever that she had suffered as she claimed.[5] Norman Swan, health reporter for Radio National, declared on Media Watch in relation to the Gibson case that 'The general rule in health and medical journalism is the same as any other form of journalism, if it sounds too good to be true it usually is.'[6] The wellness blogger and cancer survivor had been found out, but only after a number of people had been taken on an unwholesome ride.

Gibson, then, had to be punished. She was interviewed at length in the *Australian Women's Weekly* in May 2015. The contrast between her angelic appearance and her alleged mendacity was striking to the journalist who interviewed her. Clair Weaver asked 'is this young

---

4   'Charity money promised by "inspirational" health app developer Belle Gibson not handed over', *Sydney Morning Herald*, 8 March 2015, www.smh.com.au/digital-life/digital-life-news/charity-money-promised-by-inspirational-health-app-developer-belle-gibson-not-handed-over-20150306-13xgqk.html.

5   'Mega-blogger Belle Gibson casts doubt on her own cancer claims', *The Australian*, 10 March 2015, www.theaustralian.com.au/business/megablogger-belle-gibson-casts-doubt-on-her-own-cancer-claims/news-story/de179f2f17de51d1071096eb7bd2bdee.

6   'How the media fell for Belle', *Media Watch*, 16 March, 2015, www.abc.net.au/mediawatch/transcripts/s4198886.htm.

woman really capable of masterminding one of the biggest hoaxes in recent history?'[7]

The apogee of her public shaming came during her *60 Minutes* interview with Tara Brown, for which Gibson was reportedly paid $45,000.[8] During this interview, Brown marshalled the arsenal of old media to tear down the winsome and weepy Gibson. Old tabloid tricks were rolled out. The story began with Brown addressing the camera with, behind her, a baleful image of Gibson and an image of her book *The Whole Pantry*. The caption read 'The Whole Hoax'.

Brown declared 'Belle Gibson is not a victim. She is a fraud.' The interview was conducted in an interrogative shot-reverse-shot style, setting up the two women as combatants. Every gotcha moment from Brown was matched with a reaction shot from Gibson, focusing on her befuddled face. The camera zoomed in, the screen faded, and the vision was accompanied by accelerating drumbeats. *60 Minutes*, of course, claimed to be unmasking the truth, but if so this was not without their rhetorical flourishes and the reported substantial cash payment to the alleged fraudster.[9]

Brown insisted, repeatedly, that Gibson declare what was true and what false. She asked whether she would be prepared to sign a statutory declaration vouching for her version of the truth. Old media stood its ground here, deploying its hackneyed editorial practices to insist upon itself as judge and jury. Tara Brown posed firm and erect at the beginning of the report. Her hair, following anchor-woman convention, did not move. She dressed as sharply as Julie Bishop, and seemed to have worked on acquiring as imposing

---

7   'Belle Gibson: The girl who conned us all', *Australian Women's Weekly*, 25 June 2015, www.aww.com.au/latest-news/real-life/belle-gibson-the-whole-story-21124.

8   'Belle Gibson promises to tell the whole truth: I have lost everything', news.com.au, www.news.com.au/entertainment/tv/belle-gibson-promises-to-tell-the-whole-truth-i-have-lost-everything/news-story/dd6e5b8b3a31d7f13b7805214332e5a5.

9   'The Whole Hoax', *60 Minutes*, June 28, 2015, http://www.9jumpin.com.au/show/60minutes/stories/2015/june/the-whole-hoax/.

a death stare as the Deputy Prime Minister. Her styling was mature corporate: she has been around the block and she will not be seduced, unlike those naïve social media youngsters (including Armytage and O'Keefe here) by Gibson's glossy vegetable shots and mane of artfully tousled hair. Just as *The Bachelorette* put Sam Frost in a soft turtle-neck jumper whenever the show's producers wanted to depict her childlike turmoil, so too was Gibson dressed in a woolly pink jumper bathing her in soft colour. Power dressed Brown, all angles, stared her down in the shot-reverse-shot corral and shredded her girlish softness with contempt: 'How can we believe anything you say now?'

60 Minutes devoted an entire hour to Brown's hard-hitting piece. We saw much vision of Gibson at the South Melbourne Market, sniffing vegetables and squeezing fruit. We saw photos of her receiving her *Cosmopolitan* award. We were treated to the aforementioned footage of Armytage and O'Keefe giving Gibson a rapturous reception on *Sunrise*. The denouement came about two thirds into the production, with a section in which Brown explored what this story meant for 'the truth'. Once again Brown framed the conversation for us. What were the stakes here? She told us of Gibson: 'She's broken the inherent trust we place in each other'. The problem is not late-capitalism, commodity fetishism, advertising culture or political spin. The problem is not tabloid media culture that elevates beautiful young women for their purity and miraculous narratives, and then punishes them harshly when it seems they are not as pure as they claimed. The problem is not, of course, that programs like *60 Minutes* regularly pay people for interviews, in order to produce their tales of truthful *60 Minutes* reporters versus lying charlatans. No, it is Gibson who has destroyed the 'inherent trust we place in each other'. That is a heavy burden for anyone to bear. Why is Gibson so bad? Brown told us that 'She sold her sob story to the world'. But *60 Minutes* was, supposedly, buying.

After Brown framed the third act, we then entered into a bizarre conversation about the nature of truth. Brown declared 'The only thing Belle can't spin is the truth' and 'Belle can't keep up with her own truth'. Finally, in her best interrogative tone and with a hint a sarcasm, she asked Gibson 'Do you accept that your reality doesn't match reality'? This is a question from another era. It should have been Ray Martin asking the question, or Jana Wendt. It should have been George Negus in his safari suit flirting with Dolly Parton or getting stuck into Arafat. The assumption behind Brown's question was that there is a real, and she knows what it is. This was a conceit that was possible in Negus' day, when the journalist swashbuckled across the world, sending visual missives back to an Australia trapped in the world of analogue TV. But if the past 15 years or so of reality television have taught us anything, it is surely that there is no such thing as reality. Reality is a trope, in which we put people in difficult situations and watch them either flounder or flourish. The dramedy *Unreal*, which satirises dating reality television, makes that very clear with its title. Reality is not real.

60 Minutes, of course, knew and knows this. The interview with Gibson reads like a last gasp of Old Media asserting its monopoly on reality. That ship has long sailed. The story about Gibson was broken by Fairfax and *The Australian*. There was nothing investigative about the 60 Minutes report. Instead, Brown put an attractive woman with mental health issues, and a clear appetite for fame, under the pump on national television. Where have we seen this before? The answer is on just about every reality television show ever made. The major difference between this episode of *60 Minutes* and your average episode of *The Bachelor* is that Gibson was paid much more handsomely for her troubles than the women who line up to receive those roses. There are scores of wellness bloggers ready to evangelise smoothies to the world. Gibson was a prophet with feet of clay, and she will not be the last person to promise the world in an acai bowl.

The *60 Minutes* expose did not tell us anything about the how of Gibson's fraud, about the credulity that enabled her to be believed and valorised. Rather, Brown's takedown revealed, yet again, the work we want the body to do in our culture. We expect purity, of both consumption and contagion of any sort. And we will punish, very severely, those who fall short. This is something well-known to any contestant on the *Biggest Loser*, forced to endure humiliating physical challenges on screen to atone for their impure corporeality.

Main

In the opening sequence to *Kitchen Cabinet*, Annabel Crabb bakes a cake. Dressed in her customary retro 1950s housedress, she deploys an array of pastel coloured implements to sift flour, separate eggs, cream and ice. The sequence is styled Country Women's Association meets Generation X hipster, part artisanal, part ironic. The big reveal at the end of the credits is that the cake she bakes is actually in the shape of the Australian Parliament. She retools the clichés of the houseproud housewife to insist on the link between the nation and food. This is the conceit of *Kitchen Cabinet*, that if we cook and eat with our politicians we will know something new about them, and something new about our democracy. The blurb for the show asks us 'Join Annabel as she gets beyond the sound bite and helps us understand the curious creature that is the Australian Politician.' Based on the very old idea that eating together is a gesture of equanimity (a memo, apparently, that Judas did not receive), Crabb cooks and breaks bread with politicians. The politician produces the main course, while Crabb arrives with dessert in hand. The prevailing tone is one of respect and bonhomie. For Crabb, the occasion of food enables also an occasion of civility, one that refuses the adversarial binaries of the two-party system.[10]

---

10 *Kitchen Cabinet*, www.abc.net.au/tv/programs/kitchen-cabinet/.

Crabb's *Kitchen* has been receiving some heat. In Season 5 of the series, she interviewed Treasurer Scott Morrison at a beach house and was treated to his 'ScoMosas', his version of a Sri Lankan appetiser. Morrison described his conversion to Sri Lankan food, recounting a trip he took to Sri Lanka with Julie Bishop to work on immigration policy when in opposition. He described eating at a 'dodgy restaurant' and staying at a sub-par hotel, without sheets and with very small towels. The horror. The food, however, was good, Morrison exclaims. And he treats Crabb to his sub-continental delicacies. As they cook and eat, Crabb asks Morrison about his childhood in suburban Sydney. Morrison describes his young years of church and citizenship, helping out his dad who was both a cop and a local politician. Morrison is firmly God and Country. But lest he seem all white bread, let's not forget he's making 'ScoMosas'.[11]

As Minister for Immigration, Scott Morrison had determinedly 'Stopped the Boats' and enforced a regime of mandatory detention for all asylum seekers who attempted to enter Australia by boat. As a result, the policies of the Abbott government had receive sharp criticisms from both the United Nations and the Australian Human Rights Commission. This had been a government happy to vilify the refugee Other and to trade on the xenophobic anxieties of Australian voters. To see Morrison laughing it up with Crabb, and garnishing his white privilege with some spicy Sri Lankan foods, was a bitter pill to swallow for some viewers. Morrison's love of Sri Lankan cuisine, combined with his seeming callow disregard for the victims of that country's policies, seemed to point to the shallowness of the Australian multicultural project. As a nation, policies are regularly pursued that trade on racist anxieties. And yet, we are not racist because we eat curries.

---

11 'Scott Morrison', *Kitchen Cabinet*, 28 October 2015 http://iview.abc.net.au/programs/kitchen-cabinet/LE1427H001S00.

Crabb's critics charged her with allowing Morrison to obfuscate the cruelty and brutality of his policies via the show's friendly format. Morrison was allowed to perform a geniality and mildness that stood in sharp contrast to his ruthless policies. It could seem an obscenity to have two such well-fed and privileged white faces chortling in a beach house over 'ScoMosas' while children suffered in detention. In response to Crabb's argument that kitchen cabinet humanises politicians, Amy McQuire wrote in *New Matilda* that:

> Crabb fundamentally misses the point of journalism. It's not about humanising those in power, it's about humanising those who are let down by those in power. But perhaps it is symptomatic of a wider problem, the fact that our most famous journalists, with the greatest platforms, now have more in common with those they are supposed to challenge, rather than those who are being let down by a corrosive political system.[12]

McQuire read *Kitchen Cabinet* as a cosy expression of our ruling class, journalist and politician alike, cooking co-conspiratorially while pretending to be on different sides. McQuire's criticisms were echoed by Sarah Keenan in *The Conversation*, who focused particularly on the relationship between food and the body politic:

> Food ostensibly serves as an apolitical social lubricant for Crabb to show politicians' human sides, but food has a political life of its own and has long served as a marker of cultural proficiency and belonging. Kitchen Cabinet's staging of 'casual' food preparation and consumption with the nation's most powerful people reproduces a culture of white Australian

---

12 'Junk food journalism: Why Annabel Crabb's Kitchen Cabinet is toxic', *The New Matilda*, 29 October 2015 https://newmatilda.com/2015/10/29/junk-food-journalism-why-annabel-crabbs-kitchen-cabinet-is-toxic/.

entitlement to master and consume any and every cultural product, regardless of who it belongs to.[13]

For Crabb, the criticisms warranted a response. She deployed her *Sydney Morning Herald* column to defend the project of her show. She suggested that programs like *Kitchen Cabinet* were much more than entertainment, but served a democratic function in bringing all voters up close and personal with their representatives. She declared:

> I don't think you can possibly separate what people are like from what they do. Political leaders – like every single one of us – are shaped by the things that have happened to them and to the people close to them. Those factors – *what they're like* – exert a considerable and usually invisible influence over the most important decisions a political leader will ever make. Namely: which issues they are going to choose to die in a ditch for, which they will pop in the too-hard basket, which they might compromise on. This is the stuff that realistically drives the political process. And fleshy, human, and deeply subjective stuff it is too. Knowing what a person is *like* is powerful. Why should it only be political journalists and insiders who get to see it?[14]

In so doing, Crabb reminded us that the personal is political, and suggested that if we want to understand our political cultures we need to make sense of their affective frames. Know the pollie, and we will know more about the world that informs their decision making, is her argument. But that is where *Kitchen Cabinet* stops, and this is the gist of the criticisms made against the show. Crabb attempts to

---

13 'Recipes for racism: Kitchen Cabinet and the politics of racism', *The Conversation*, 12 November 2015 https://theconversation.com/recipes-for-racism-kitchen-cabinet-and-the-politics-of-food-50516.

14 'Kitchen Cabinet: Appetite for justice fuels unjust desserts', *Sydney Morning Herald*, 7 November 2015, www.smh.com.au/comment/kitchen-cabinet-when-policy-combats-off-the-menu-20151106-gksnir.html.

reveal the human wielding the whisk, but she does not push them to explain that humanity in relation to the policies they implement. How does Morrison go from 'ScoMosas' to children in detention?

Dessert

The Katering Show was a web series that emerged in 2015, and went viral. It has since been picked up by the ABC. Hosted by two very funny Kates – McClennan and McCartney – the series of short episodes satirised food culture in Australia. The most shared episode was that which examined the Thermomix, the $3000 German appliance that inspires extraordinary devotion in its owners, and befuddlement in the rest of us. As they said of the appliance, 'it's something that you buy for yourself because you've always wanted to join a cult, but you don't have the energy for group sex'.[15] Their targets also included quitting sugar, organics, farmer's markets, paleo and the racism that occurs when 'ethnic' food cultures are appropriated by the white imaginary. In the first episode, when explaining the premise of the show, Kate McClennan explains that Kate McCartney has been diagnosed with a number of food allergies, which preclude her from eating a number of things. *The Katering Show* will explore how Kate McCartney can keep herself healthy, but also still cook enjoyable food. Kate McClennan explains why this is necessary, why it is a problem that her friend must have such a restricted diet: 'She was missing out on the food culture revolution that was happening all around her. Street food, raw food, cooked food, food porn, regular porn. She was missing out on all of it'.[16]

The 'food culture revolution', as the Kates imply, is a joke. If a revolution is an overturning, then our televisual food cultures do nothing of the sort. Rather, food on screen in Australia reinforces the

---

15 'The Katering Show: Thermomix', www.youtube.com/watch?v=4yr_etbfZtQ.
16 'The Katering Show: Mexicana Festiana', https://youtu.be/J55vgxNaaBY

bourgeois imaginary, accommodating difference as long as it conforms to the genre of a freshly sourced food dream. Food in this context does not bring us together, or enable us to embrace our differences. It is the object through which we fantasise cosmopolitanism, within a polity that fails to deliver it.

Chapter 3

Broadcasting Disruption

Mark Hearn

In his first press conference after taking the Liberal Party leadership from Prime Minister Tony Abbott on 14 September 2015 Malcolm Turnbull asserted that "we have to recognise that the disruption that we see driven by technology, the volatility in change is our friend … The Australia of the future has to be a nation that is agile, that is innovative, that is creative".[1]

Turnbull's disruption named a force that reflected technological change and which has been reshaping Australian society for several decades. Historian Daniel Rodgers has described the late twentieth century as an age of fracture: "imagined collectivities shrank; notions of structure and power thinned out." New technologies destabilised familiar patterns of work, social organisation and ideology.[2]

In Australia, these patterns accelerated in the new century, intensifying economic production, promoting a culture of individualisation – with a tendency to degenerate into dismal soap opera – and disabling the Australian labour movement. These powerful disruptions were vividly illustrated in three programs broadcast by the ABC in 2015.

The politics of *The Killing Season* (*TKS*) was a product of the age of disruption; *Making Australia Great* (*MAG*) described its political economy. An episode of the current affairs program *Four Corners*

---

1 'Transcript: Vote on the Liberal Party Leadership, 15 September 2015, Malcolm Turnbull MP', www.malcolmturnbull.com.au/media/transcript-vote-on-the-liberal-party-leadership

2 Daniel T. Rodgers, *Age of Fracture*, Harvard University Press, 2012, p.3; Hartmut Rosa, *Alienation and Acceleration*, NSU Press, Malmo, 2010, pp.20, 45.

focusing on allegations of corruption and inappropriate conduct by former Health Services Union federal secretary Kathy Jackson and her partner, Fair Work Australia Vice President Michael Lawler, provided a brutal illustration of disruption in personal lives.

The ignoble public dismembering of Kathy Jackson's career is in part a product of the failure of the union movement to make the necessary structural and ethical adaptations to the age of disruption, a failure extending back to the 1980s. As the Australian economy was transformed – and the Hawke and Keating governments and the trade union movement played a leading role in driving the change – the labour movement itself failed to transform.[3] *TKS* and *Four Corners* documented the consequences.

Making Australia Great

That Australia has experienced transformative disruption since the 1980s excited *MAG* presenter and writer George Megalogenis. Screened on ABC1 in three primetime episodes across March 2015, *MAG* sought to explain Australia's long boom since the early 1990s and the opportunities it offers for forging, as Megalogenis hopes, a truly great nation.[4] A former Canberra press gallery journalist, Megalogenis is an enthusiastic evangelist for this cause, reflected in two impressive book-length studies of contemporary politics including *The Australian Moment*, of which *MAG* is essentially a TV companion piece.[5] By greatness Megalogenis primarily means economic performance. *MAG* deftly accounts for the adaptability of

---

3   Kerrie Saville, 'The Structural Events Approach – A "Better" Way to Understand Long-term Change in Trade Union Structure: The Australian Story (1986 – 96)', *Journal of Industrial Relations*, Vol. 49, November 2007, p.770.

4   *Making Australia Great*, ABC 1, Episode 1 'Bad Hair Decades', Tuesday 17 March 2015, 8:30 pm; Episode 2 'Growing Pains', Tuesday 24 March 2015, 8:30 pm; Episode 3 'Australia's Second Chance', Tuesday 31 March, 8.30 pm.

5   George Megalogenis, *The Longest Decade*, Scribe, Melbourne, 2006; George Megalogenis, *The Australian Moment*, Penguin, Melbourne, 2012.

governments in the 1980s and 1990s to adjust the Australian economy to the new conditions of globalisation, imposed by the breakdown of Bretton Woods financial regulation, the end of the Cold War, the shift to Thatcherism and Reaganomics and the increasing impact of new technology.

It's all crisply visualised in familiar terms: chalk board stock market scribblers in the early period give way, as the three episodes proceed from the 1970s towards the present, to computer screens and bright digital representations of graphs and numbers, interspersed with a familiar retinue of talking heads – primarily politicians, interspersed with figures from business and the public service; few union leaders appear.

MAG's visualisations reflect the point made by cultural studies scholar Graeme Turner that business reporting in the media vastly expanded in the 1980s and "turned business into a spectacle".[6] The *MAG* viewer is often invited to marvel at a spectacle of dynamic growth.

A compelling optimist, there is a touch of Dr Pangloss about George Megalogenis's determination to celebrate Australia's incipient greatness. "I want to talk to the decision makers … I want to go beyond the fog of politics to see Australia as it really is … Can we make something of this moment?" Yet by talking to the decision makers Megalogenis tended to immerse himself in the fog of politics, or at least in the self-justifying rationales of former Prime Ministers and Treasurers.

Tracking a whiggish path of progress from the 1970s onward Megalogenis obscures the negative stimuli that compelled response and generated disruption. The 1983 floating of the dollar is presented symbolically as a stroke of bold innovation, a big bang moment that unleashed the future. The dollar float responded to pressure

6   Graeme Turner, *Making it National: Nationalism and Australian Popular Culture*, St Leonards, Allen & Unwin, 1994, p.18.

of circumstance over which Australia exerted little control: the collapse of Bretton Woods and the 1970s Oil Shocks set in train the global financial instability that pitched the Australian economy into turbulence.[7]

New technology also contributed to the float decision: as Paul Kelly observes, the pressure on the Australian dollar intensified over the late 1970s and early 1980s as computerisation accelerated the global transfer of capital and increased Australia's exposure to opportunistic trading in the dollar. The float was in some ways a reactive leap into the unknown with both positive and negative consequences.[8]

Yet Megalogenis is right to note the benefits that flowed from the economic reforms of the 1980s. That former treasurer Peter Costello could remind *MAG* viewers that no Australian bank sustained a single financial quarterly loss as a consequence of the 2007–08 Global Financial Crisis, while over 500 banks around the world collapsed, is a striking testament to the adaptability built into Australian political economy from the Hawke-Keating era.

That Australia had the fiscal resources to meet the challenge of the GFC, and has enjoyed twenty-one years of unbroken economic growth since the recession of the early 1990s, may not necessarily reflect the greatness of Australian society, but it is an achievement. It was a story that attracted respectable popular attention: focusing on the GFC earned *MAG* its highest ratings – episode three ranked ninth for free-to-air evening viewing on 31 March.[9]

MAG concludes by connecting economic and social openness in a cascade of images celebrating Australian ethnic diversity. Megalogenis contentedly strolled through a multicultural festival in his Melbourne home town: "We make our luck when we run an open

---

7   Tony Judt, *Postwar*, Vintage Books, London, 2010, ch.XIV; Ed Conway, *The Summit*, Little, Brown, London, 2014, ch.16.

8   Paul Kelly, *The End of Certainty*, Allen and Unwin, Sydney, 1992, p.79.

9   *Courier Mail*, 1 April 2015.

economy and an open migration program". "We have to build for a big Australia", he argues; to continue to prosper Australia must aim for a population of between 30–50 million by the mid-twenty-first century, "because this is the sort of population that comes from being the last rich nation standing". This 'populate or perish' assertion is a familiar cry from the old days of Australia Unlimited in the 1920s, and nearly a century later may remain a wistful and even dubious hope. True to *MAG's* narrative form, this optimistic population claim – and whether it is either sustainable or desirable – is allowed to stand unchallenged.[10]

The problem with *MAG* is its stark absences. There is little focus on the negative aspects of deregulation – the casualisation of the workforce, the growing divide between rich and poor, the victimisation of welfare recipients through overbearing surveillance and punitive measures.[11] Megalogenis barely registers the debate over Howard's Work Choices industrial relations reforms, yet this debate in the period 2005–7 brought into focus the sharp divide of economic growth: how are the rewards of productivity to be distributed? Who rules in the workplace? Should managers enjoy an unfettered prerogative?

Megalogenis sidesteps the cravenly divided politics that form the subject of *TKS*: he notes the collapse into the rancorous Rudd-Gillard-Abbott period in a vague generalisation. It is hard to imagine a truly great nation producing such a wretchedly paralysed political culture. Or perhaps the same disruptions that produced profound and rapid economic change have also generated Killing Season politics?

---

10   Stuart Macintyre, *The Oxford History of Australia*, Oxford University Press, Melbourne, 1986, Vol. 4, p.198.
11   Andrew Leigh, *Battlers and Billionaires: The Story of Inequality in Australia*, Redback, Melbourne, 2013.

The Killing Season

Besotted with personality politics *TKS* also struggles to account for the causes of disruption. *TKS* replicated the media cult of personality and the hothouse narcissism of parliament house politics, evident in the bleak, black and white title frames focused around a pensively posed Gillard silhouette backlit by the looming, starkly bleached image of Rudd's face. At 8.30 pm each Tuesday for three weeks in June 2015 the insistent melancholy of the andante movement of Schubert's Piano Trio No.2 signalled another ABC1 episode of spite, revenge and hubris triumphing over nation building.[12]

The Kevin Rudd-Julia Gillard leadership team emerged in 2006 because it seemed a solution to Labor's dilemmas, filling a personality and communicative vacuum, although perhaps not addressing a substantial policy and philosophical absence as the labour movement struggled to define a new ideology and organisational practice to adapt to a post-industrial world.[13]

As Opposition leader Kevin Rudd offered the possibility of re-newal, and developed as an effective challenger to Prime Minister John Howard's government. Yet in many respects Rudd proved more a symptom of Labor's dilemmas than a solution. The most telling comment on the illusory nature of Rudd's appeal in *TKS* was provided by Labor MP Tony Burke. Observing Rudd's electioneering skills during the 2007 campaign, Burke was awestruck at his leader's chameleon facility to engage with diverse audiences: "He'd be joking

---

12 *The Killing Season*, ABC 1, Episode 1 'The Prime Minister and his Loyal Deputy (2006–2009)', Tuesday 9 June 2015, 8:30 pm; Episode 2 'Great Moral Challenge (2009–2010)'; Tuesday 16 June 2015, 8:30 pm; Episode 3 'The Long Shadow (2010–2013)', Tuesday 23 June 2015, 8.30 pm.

13 Martin Painter, 'Economic Policy, Market Liberalism and the "End of Australian Politics"', *Australian Journal of Political Science*, Vol. 31, No. 3, 1996; Ashley Lavelle, *The Death of Social Democracy, Political Consequences in the 21st Century*, Ashgate, 2008.

around with [Liberal MP] Joe Hockey on *Sunrise* and by night he'd be talking foreign policy on *Lateline*. You had somebody who was just spanning every aspect of communications that no other politician in the country could". Labor of course won convincingly and Howard lost his own seat in Parliament.[14]

TKS captures Kevin07 effortlessly engaging with the people in street walks and selfies; he was a postmodern mimic who could convincingly tell a variety of audiences what they wanted to hear. Rudd's astute election claim to be an "economic conservative" was not so much a policy stance as a media performance, signalling to commentators and the public that he would conform to the prevailing narrative of Australian political economy.

As PM Rudd was sensitive to Labor's inclusive spirit, represented in the apology to the Stolen Generations on 12 February 2008. Rudd also demonstrated acute foresight about the looming impact of the GFC, as Treasury Secretary Ken Henry attested in both *MAG* and *TKS*: Rudd's leadership was decisive in formulating an effective government response and ensuring that Australians did not experience the economic crisis.

Yet from 2009 and into 2010 Rudd apparently became increasingly indecisive. As both Rudd's popularity and Labor's position in the opinion polls collapsed, and as the government wallowed from one policy misstep to the next – over asylum seekers, the response to climate change and the mining tax – Rudd seemed immobilised, unable to link glib script with substantial outcome.[15]

Embarking on a seemingly endless tour of hospitals around Australia, as *TKS* records in a blizzard of edited images of corridor walks, meet and greets and encouraging bedside chats, Rudd, dragging

---

14 Christine Jackman, *Inside Kevin07: The People, the Plan, the Prize*, Melbourne University Publishing, Carlton, 2008.

15 David Marr, *Power Trip: The Political Journey of Kevin Rudd*, Black Inc., Melbourne, 2010.

despairing Health Minister Nicola Roxon with him, avoiding the pressing need to formulate a coherent health policy.

Meanwhile Opposition Leader Tony Abbott hammered the drumbeat of simplistic and debilitating political attacks on the government, promising if elected to 'stop the boats' of desperate asylum seekers regularly arriving off Australia's north western coast. Fearing Abbott's ascendancy in the polls, *TKS* reports, Labor's factional bosses and the operatives in the federal Labor caucus suffered less hesitation than Rudd. These factional operatives are the often the 'stars' of the program. They were the killers, prone to lamenting their function and basking in the professional pleasure of the kill.

In *TKS* the caucus faction leaders seemingly delighted in recounting their participation in the lightning strike that brought down Kevin Rudd in the space of a single evening. Julia Gillard's abrupt replacement of Rudd as prime minister in an uncontested ballot on 24 June 2010 stunned the nation, and most cabinet ministers, who had no idea that a coup was underway.

Where had the killers come from, and what motivated them? Factional operatives, privileging polls, were provided with an ascendancy born of the same dynamic that generated Kevin07: filling Labor's philosophical and policy vacuum not with conviction but process and slogan. Unable to be steadied by the inner resource of self-belief and clear purpose, Labor became all hypersensitive surface, prone to panicked response to the neurotic stimulus of polls and focus groups. Frustrated ambitions found justification in Rudd's failings.

Several of the factional operators recreated their coup roles for *TKS*, intensifying the impression of politics as crass and superficial reality TV game. Self-parody began on the night of the coup and continued in *TKS*, including then junior minister Bill Shorten's Vietnamese restaurant mobile phone number-crunching antics. Available footage did not require Shorten to re-enact his vote gathering for Gillard.

Senator Sam Dastyari from the New South Wales Labor Right faction helpfully re-played receiving news of bad polling in four New South Wales marginal seats, which proved decisive in providing justification for Rudd's removal. In *TKS* Dastyari is filmed on a busy city street as he breathlessly and self-referentially recreates his caller's despair: "Dasher it's worse than bad: we're bloody stuffed". 'Dasher' holds a mobile phone model to his ear that did not exist in June 2010, somewhat dispelling the illusion of verisimilitude.

Self-satisfaction is embodied in another Labor senator from the factional Right, Mark Bishop, who asserted of the Rudd kill: "In terms of its professional execution, you'd have to say it was the best". In *TKS* Bishop recounts how he soon changed his mind and made overtures to the displaced and aggrieved Rudd, offering to help him metaphorically kill his replacement, Julia Gillard.

Under the forensic probing of *TKS* presenter and interviewer Sarah Ferguson, Gillard struggled to convincingly justify the coup or deny that she had prior knowledge of the plotter's intrigues, despite her key role in the government as deputy prime minister. Gillard's terse assertion that by early 2010 Rudd was "personally miserable … politically immobilised" smacked of a tidy post-coup rationalisation.

Ferguson's questioning also exposed Rudd's evasive justifications of the leaks of cabinet deliberations that undermined Gillard during the August 2010 election campaign. Labor's support collapsed and it was forced into minority government. As cabinet minister Greg Combet noted in *TKS*, Gillard's lack of campaign experience as leader also told against Labor, evident in her awkward offer to reveal the "real Julia", an attempt to regain campaign control through a stronger personal connection with voters that only focused attention on "character issues".

TKS offered a grim visualisation of Labor's post-coup divisions: the dismal image of an almost empty Melbourne convention centre on election night as Gillard glumly conceded that a final outcome required tortuous days of vote counting. Gillard's press secretary Sean Kelly described the event as "a poorly attended funeral".

In an attempt to secure support from the Greens for the minority government Gillard reneged on her election promise not to introduce a price on carbon and rashly compounded this problem by allowing the policy to be identified as a 'carbon tax.' In *TKS* Wayne Swan, Treasurer in the Rudd and Gillard governments, observed that as a consequence Labor lost control of the climate change policy debate and gave Tony Abbott another line of simplistic, sloganeering attack.

In Parliament the minority government functioned well, passing over 250 pieces of legislation and significant reforms in disability care and education. As PM Julia Gillard found that she was better suited to managing process than strategy and inspiring the Australian people to support her cause – and what was that cause? Gillard struggled and indeed dismissed the need to articulate a narrative of her governing. It could be said she failed to offer voters a reason to believe in her and the government.[16]

Gillard's enemies constructed a narrative for her: 'Juliar' the Lady Macbeth witch, misleading voters over the carbon tax, executing an elected PM, and perhaps worst of all being a woman. *TKS* offered graphic evidence of the debased assault on Gillard's gender, character, family, and her physical appearance, that has no equal precedent in Australian political life. Tony Abbott's gleeful participation in barely rational public protests – or hate sessions – directed at Gillard, reflected the depth of Abbott's willingness to cynically divide Australians in his own political interest. Perhaps the most poignant illustration of the emotional impact of this vilification in *TKS* are scenes of Gillard government Trade Minister Craig Emerson in tearful disbelief that the standard of public life could sink so low.[17]

---

16 Michael Cooney, *The Gillard Project*, Viking, Melbourne, 2015.

17 Samantha Trenoweth ed., *Bewitched & Bedevilled: Women Write the Gillard Years*, Hardie Grant Books, Richmond, 2013.

TKS observes that Abbott's connivance in the shock-jock and News Limited assaults on Gillard culminated in the 9 October 2012 exchange in Parliament as Abbott slyly parroted broadcaster's Alan Jones claim that Gillard's recently deceased father would have been ashamed of her: Abbott asserted the government should die of shame for it failings. Gillard responded with the controlled rage of the misogyny speech; as *TKS* records, Gillard never spoke more powerfully or eloquently. Abbott proved impervious to his own shaming, leading the Coalition to election victory on 7 September 2013.

TKS recounts the tawdry details of the claustrophobic caucus intrigue that led to the collapse of the Labor government and Rudd's defeat of Gillard in a leadership challenge on 26 June 2013. It is sufficient to echo frontbencher Anthony Albanese's rueful observation, made on the occasion of the 2010 coup, that executing Rudd proved an efficient way of killing two Labor Prime Ministers in one fell stroke.[18]

TKS records a claim by Craig Emerson that he coined the phrase 'the killing season' to describe the dangerous weeks when plotters sense an opportunity to strike down a failing leader before Parliament rises for the long winter recess. Whether or not there is really an identifiable phenomenon as 'the killing season' is beside the point: it lives as a legend attractive to politicians and journalists and their sense of inhabiting a vital drama, and which may be recreated as entertainment. The appeal of a killing season may not be wholly evident to a bemused public: the program rated well for the ABC but could not match the popularity of MasterChef.[19]

---

18 Kerry-Anne Walsh, *The Stalking of Julia Gillard: How the Media and Team Rudd Contrived to Bring Down the Prime Minister*, Allen & Unwin, Sydney, 2013.

19 *Sydney Morning Herald*, 17 June 2015.

Four Corners: 'Inside the Eye of the Storm'

Neither could *Four Corners'* morbid focus on Kathy Jackson and Michael Lawler, 'Inside the eye of the storm', overcome the appeal of *The X Factor*, although it 'nabbed' the next day's news headlines, making it 'a good Monday for the ABC', according to *TV Tonight*.[20] Watching the breakdown of two human beings on television makes for the kind of entertaining torment enjoyed by both mainstream and social media. It turns victims into their own self-consuming predators. *TKS* offered such spectacle on a scale of national theatre; *Four Corners* reduced the focus to a kitchen melodrama, filmed in the couple's 'retreat' on the New South Wales south coast and broadcast in the primetime 8.30 pm slot on 19 October 2015.[21]

Barely a fortnight after the ABC lavished program time promoting Mental Health Week, Kathy Jackson, by *Four Corners'* own admission in a state of distress, requiring daily professional psychological care, was nonetheless subject to intrusive focus by the camera. This concentration was most punishing and 'revealing' not in the trite denials of personal responsibility recorded in the interviews with Jackson – the interviews added nothing new to the public record – but in the silent focus on her distressed face, or seated alone at a verandah table, head in hands and her back to the camera. Kathy Jackson may be guilty of criminal offences and abusing the trust of the workers she represented. If so, her punishment began under the gaze of the camera.

Michael Lawler's video diary, offered as a highlight of the *Four Corners* focus on the couple, seemed a prolonged five hour 'selfie', his array of pliable and mannered facial gestures as revealing as his conspiratorial rationales. *Four Corners* claimed that showcasing Lawler's

---

20   *TV Tonight*, 20 October 2015, www.tvtonight.com.au/2015/10/four-corners-interview-nabs-headlines-on-good-monday-for-abc.html.

21   *Four Corners*, 'Jackson and Lawler – inside the eye of the storm', ABC 1, Monday 19 October 2015, 8.30 pm.

diary performance and taped conversations with others was justified by stunning revelations. The most *Four Corners* extracted was Lawler's boss apparently assuring Lawler that his sick leave could be unlimited, when the same boss had said publicly that that was not the case. This underwhelming revelation was also an exposure of Lawler's self-obsession; it was merely a by-product of the possible entrapment that he seems to have been preoccupied with for several years.

Media headlines following the broadcast manufactured a 'controversy' (this being part of the effect current affairs programs like *Four Corners* seek) over Lawler's use of an ugly expletive, "cunt-struck", to describe how his relationship with Jackson may be perceived in the public domain. What was most revealing was the guileless deployment of the derogatory term: Lawler simply said it in passing, without emphasis and apparently without thought for its impact on its subject – Jackson – or how its use might make him appear to the audience.

Established in 1961, *Four Corners* has been and remains an outstanding product of traditional current affairs television. In this episode it revealed its own struggle to negotiate the ethical traps of the digital age, replicating the predations of social media. All Jackson and Lawler revealed was a woman and man at the centre of their own crisis. *Four Corners* failed to probe how Jackson's behaviour, and that of other senior officials of the Health Services Union, may be a product of insular trade union cultures which lack effective systems of accountability, as claimed by the Royal Commission into Trade Union Governance and Corruption, whose hearings provided another media spectacle in 2015.[22]

Disruption is also replicated in the rapid visual edits of *TKS* and *MAG*, reflecting the welter of information that both the public and politicians are required to filter; a disoriented reflex we have normalised. It is reflected further in the politics of the 24-hour news

---

22 'Dyson Heydon's Royal Commision exposes corrupt union deals', *Australian*, 22 August 2015.

cycle, which *TKS* amplified as drama. Perhaps this is why the *Sydney Morning Herald's* entertainment reporter observed that if the 'political reality' of *MAG* proved too much, viewers could resort to the American sit-com *The Big Bang Theory*, screening in the same timeslot on the rival Nine Network.[23]

MAG showed us how the news cycle intensified, at least in the broad process of economic and information acceleration at work since the 1970s: the political economy of disaggregation, with individualism privileged at the expense of collective forms of identity. In the age of disruption we are encouraged to believe that we must fall back on our own resources: masters of our self-government, entrepreneurs in the workplace and in the management of our personal lives.[24] Kathy Jackson and Michael Lawler, an "embattled power couple", according to *TV Tonight*, received a harsh lesson in personal responsibility, cast adrift in the media gaze.[25] Their public melodrama, and that which reduced the careers of two Labor Prime Ministers to vilification and farce, are sensational manifestations of the fate of lives disrupted in the quest to make Australia great.

23 *SMH*, 16 March 2015.

24 Nikolas Rose, *Powers of Freedom*, Cambridge University Press, Cambridge, 1999, pp.142–145, 156.

25 *TV Tonight*, 20 October, 2015 http://www.tvtonight.com.au/2015/10/four-corners-interview-nabs-headlines-on-good-monday-for-abc.html.

CHAPTER 4

Anzac on TV

CAROLYN HOLBROOK

The centenary of the landing of Australian soldiers on a remote Turkish peninsula on 25 April 1915 was a perfect storm of nationalist pride and commercial opportunity. Australians were invited to indulge our patriotism and produce our credit cards, often simultaneously. We could cruise to Gallipoli in remembrance of the Anzacs, with Bert Newton and Daryl Braithwaite head-lining the on-board entertainment, or sleep under 'the same stars that the Anzacs slept under one hundred years ago' at Camp Gallipoli.[1] We could 'raise a glass' of Victoria Bitter beer in tribute to the Anzacs, with the sanction of the Commonwealth government and the RSL.[2] Women were invited to adorn their kitchens with Flanders poppy oven mitts and themselves with poppy earrings and aprons. The *World War One Commemorative Cook Book* offered 'a culinary journey through the period when the ANZAC legend was born', with 'tantalising' dishes such as Roo Tail Stew, Turkish Delight and Harissa Spiced Backstrap Salad.[3] Blokes could wear poppy cuff links, Rising Sun signet rings

---

1   Gallipoli Cruise 2015, www.guideposttours.com.au/util/doc.jsp?n=Gallipoli-ANZAC-Cruise-2015-Excursions-Activities_131726662497380.PDF, accessed 20 November 2015. Camp Gallipoli, www.campgallipoli.com.au/, accessed 20 November 2015.

2   Raise a Glass Appeal, www.raiseaglass.com.au/age-gate.php, accessed 20 November 2015. Commonwealth legislation governs the use of the word 'Anzac'. Carlton and United Breweries is permitted to use the word 'Anzac' in its advertising by the Department of Veterans' Affairs and the RSL because it donates $1 million each year to the RSL and Legacy.

3   David Hopgood, *World War One Commemorative Cook Book: A Culinary Journey Through Our Military History*, Big Sky Publishing, Sydney, 2014,

48

and T-shirts proclaiming 'Lest We Forget' and 'I ♥ ANZAC'.[4] They could collect bits of well-pedigreed pine tree whittled into coasters, lapel pins and letter openers.[5] Parents could tuck their kids into bed with cuddly toys called Anzac Ted, Nurse Florence, Murphy the Donkey and Sarbi the Explosives Detection Dog.

Our television screens were not immune from the Anzac rush. The one hundredth anniversary of the beach landing that spawned the nation's favourite legend had all the makings of a 'broadcasting bonanza'.[6] Yet, despite the high hopes of broadcasters and advertisers, Anzac-themed television shows failed conspicuously to excite the public imagination in 2015. Ratings for expensive dramas and documentaries were poor, as viewers preferred cheaply produced reality television shows. Journalists and academics began to speculate that Australians were suffering from 'Gallipoli fatigue' – a reaction against the ubiquity of the Anzac story in popular culture. This chapter traces the fortunes of Anzac television during 2015, with a particular focus on Channel Nine's seven part series *Gallipoli*. It argues that Australians are not so much fatigued by Gallipoli as discerning about the forms in which they consume it. The failure of Anzac television in 2015 demonstrates the disjunction between mythology and history; the popularity of the Anzac legend is *not* underwritten by an abiding popular interest in the story behind it.

---

www.bigskypublishing.com.au/Books/Military/World-War-1-Commemorative-Cookbook/1058/productview.aspx, accessed 20 November 2015.

4   Signet Ring at Webstore, www.webstore.com/item,pgr,George-Crown-Rising-Sun-1915-2015-Commemorative-Ring,name,51554367,auction_id,auction_details, accessed 20 November 2015. A selection of T-shirts can be found at Zazzle, www.zazzle.com.au/anzac+tshirts, accessed 20 November 2015.

5   Australian War Memorial online shop, www.raiseaglass.com.au/age-gate.php, accessed 20 November 2015.

6   Andrew Hornery, 'Stars Pulled as Networks Get Cold Feet on Gallipoli', 17 April 2015, www.smh.com.au/lifestyle/private-sydney/private-sydney-stars-pulled-as-networks-get-cold-feet-on-gallipoli-20150415-1mm4z4.html, accessed 13 November 2015.

Television executives had ample justification for scheduling a bumper year of Anzac programming. There was no doubting the public appetite for Anzac; since the 1990s crowds at dawn services and marches, both in Australia and overseas, had continued to swell. Forty-two thousand people applied for the ballot to allocate just 3860 double tickets for the Gallipoli dawn service in 2015.[7] Anzac was popular with young Australians and women: the typical attendee at the Gallipoli dawn service was a woman in her late twenties.[8] This statistic would have pleased commercial television executives keen to attract the 16–39 year old demographic coveted by their advertisers. There were other financial incentives. About $4 million of the approximately $530 million that is being spent on Great War commemoration by Australian governments was direct-ed to television and other arts productions.[9] In addition to the $4 million of Anzac centenary funding, Screen Australia would con-tribute almost $7 million to television dramas and documentaries with Anzac themes.[10]

The ABC was the most prolific producer of Anzac television. It kicked off the 'bonanza' in August 2014 with a six-part series called *Anzac Girls*, which told the stories of five Australian nurses of the Great War.[11] *The War that Changed Us* also debuted in August 2014;

---

7   Lisa Cox, 'Ballot for Passes to Anzac Centenary Commemorations at Gallipoli Now Complete', 16 April 2015, www.smh.com.au/federal-politics/political-news/ballot-for-passes-to-anzac-centenary-commemorations-at-gallipoli-now-complete-20150416-1mm5lm.html, accessed 21 November 2015.

8   For statistic, Cox, ibid.

9   For the latest figures on how much Australia spending on Great War commemoration compared to other nations, see Honest History, www.honesthistory.net.au, accessed 27 November 2015.

10   Justin Burke, 'Patriotic Drama: Arts Undaunted by Anzac Fatigue', *Australian*, 18 April 2015, www.theaustralian.com.au/arts/review/patriotic-drama-arts-undaunted-by-anzac-fatigue/story-fn9n8gph-1227306693792?memtype=anonym ous, accessed 4 November 2015.

11   Hornery, op cit.

a sophisticated documentary-drama that examined the Australian experience of war through the eyes of several protagonists. The ABC aired three documentaries in April 2015. *Lest We Forget What?*, directed by Rachel Landers and presented by young Sydney journalist Kate Aubusson, trained a spotlight on the unthinking acceptance of the Anzac legend by young Australians. Sam Neill's *Why Anzac?* was an equally intelligent exploration of Anzac mythology drawing on the actor's own family history. And *Australia's Great Warhorse* shifted the focus from Anzac mythology to the 130,000 horses who served with Australian troops in the Middle East.

Channel Seven, which is owned by the chairman of the Australian War Memorial council Kerry Stokes, was home to the most chest-beating of the Anzac productions. Its two-part series about Australians who won the Victoria Cross at Gallipoli was hosted by Ben Roberts-Smith, who himself won a Victoria Cross in 2012 for rushing an enemy machine gun post in Afghanistan. *Gallipoli: The Power of Ten* featured intricate re-enactments of the events that earned men such as Albert Jacka, John Hamilton and Alfred Shout their decorations. Like Stokes, Roberts-Smith is an Anzac enthusiast who counts the men in the series as heroes and the Turkish territory in which they fought as 'our nation's Sacred Ground'.[12]

Channel Ten was the least enthusiastic of the free-to-air channels, opting for a low-budget series of 'mini-documentaries' called *The First Anzacs*, in which well-known actors read the letters and diaries of prominent figures from the Great War.[13] Foxtel, on the other hand, made a major investment in a four-hour long drama called *Deadline Gallipoli*. The series found an original angle on a well-known story, examining the experience of four journalists who covered the

---

12   Ben Roberts-Smith, 'The Power of One: Watch Part One', 20 April 2015, https://au.news.yahoo.com/sunday-night/features/a/27065343/the-power-of-ten-an-exclusive-look-at-our-vc-heroes/, accessed 25 November 2015.

13   The First Anzacs, Channel Ten, http://tenplay.com.au/channel-ten/the-first-anzacs, accessed 9 November 2015.

campaign; Englishman Ellis Ashmead Bartlett and Australians Charles Bean, Phillip Schuler and Keith Murdoch. Sam Worthington, who played Schuler, brought star power to a stellar production, whose themes of war reportage, truth-telling and propaganda remained as pertinent in 2015 as they were one hundred years earlier.

Of the commercial television stations, Channel Nine made the biggest financial investment in the Anzac centenary. The network's Sunday night flagship show *60 Minutes* told the 'Lost Stories of Anzac'. The formula was well-worn; personal stories and hitherto 'hidden' sources caked in layers of hyperbole and manipulated emotion – "For one hundred years these stories have been kept secret, until now … [meet] the Aussie families who will be changed forever by the secrets of Anzac", shouted the promotion. Nine also boasted the undoubted star of Anzac-themed television in 2015. *Gallipoli* was a $15 million, eight-hour long series produced by Endemol, three years in the making.[14] With a cast of 150 actors and 700 extras, it was filmed over sixty-nine days in Werribee, Point Cook and Bacchus Marsh, west of Melbourne and at Mount Eliza, south east of Melbourne.

Gallipoli tells the story of the campaign from the perspective of Tolly Johnson, played by 17-year-old, Adelaide-born actor Kodi Smit-McPhee. At 17, Tolly is too young to enlist, but lies about his age so he can join his older brother Bevan in the great adventure. Both are among the first wave of troops to land at Gallipoli. The script by Christopher Lee was particularly influenced by Les Carlyon's book

---

14   Emma Reynolds, 'The Story That Made Liz Hayes Cry: Teenager Lured to His Death in Gallipoli', 2 March 2015, www.news.com.au/entertainment/tv/the-story-that-made-liz-hayes-cry-teenager-lured-to-his-death-in-gallipoli/news-stor y/1d2f4ee00dd1e726660d2e1945c949ef, accessed 25 November 2015. 'Australia's Biggest Stars on Frontline as TV Networks to Fight with Competing Gallipoli Dramas', news.com.au, 25 April 2014, http://www.news.com.au/entertainment/movies/australias-biggest-stars-on-frontline-as-tv-networks-to-fight-with-competing-gallipoli-dramas/story-fnk850z8-1226895066506, accessed 11 November 2015.

Gallipoli, which has sold well over 100,000 copies since it was first published in 2001.[15] After reading widely about the campaign – '25 books in toto' – Lee considered Carlyon's 'the finest Australian work on the campaign as a whole'.[16] Executive producer John Edwards shared Lee's admiration for Carlyon's *Gallipoli*: "because it's a complete history of Gallipoli, but also an intensely poetic, personal and humane one. And it was the poetry of it that really attracted us".[17]

Lee was born in 1947 and, like so many of his generation, joined in the radical activism of the 1960s. Yet, unlike many of his peers, he did not connect protest against the Vietnam War with hostility towards Anzac commemoration:

> As a university student I attended many anti-war demonstrations. It was kind of what you did in those long-haired days. But my view (inasmuch as I took a political stance) was anti-the Vietnam adventure, not anti-war as such. My vague view of Gallipoli was from my middle-class Anglo upbringing (a great uncle was a stretcher-bearer on the peninsula) so, (like most of my demonstrating peers) I was never aware of being anti-Anzac as such. Anzac Day didn't resonate with us. It was seen as the *One Day of the Year* when old soldiers got drunk and played two-up. But the Anzacs – particularly the men of Gallipoli – were somehow inviolate. It was probably, even then, the power of their myth that they were untouchable.[18]

---

15 Les Carlyon, Gallipoli, Macmillan, Sydney, 2001. For book sales, Pan Macmillan Australia, www.panmacmillan.com.au/9780330426039, accessed 16 November 2015.

16 Author email correspondence with Christopher Lee, 20 November 2015.

17 John Edwards quoted in Karl Quinn, 'Cameras Roll on Gallipoli as War Stories Hit the Trenches', *Sydney Morning Herald*, www.smh.com.au/entertainment/movies/cameras-roll-on-gallipoli-as-war-stories-hit-the-trenches-20140424-zqyzy.html, accessed 17 November 2015.

18 Author email correspondence with Christopher Lee.

Lee came to the task of writing the screenplay for *Gallipoli* with strong views about the horror of war, but "not knowing anything at all" about the Gallipoli campaign itself: "and then gradually, the more I learned about it the more I started disliking the politicians and the senior generals and finding fascination in the soldiers down in the trenches".[19] He "wrote the screenplay as an anti-war work, trying to show that the Gallipoli campaign in particular and war in general, is a messy, awful business. I tried to keep the 'glory' and the 'sacrifice' of 'the fallen' and such, well out of it".[20]

Lee's anti-war views were in keeping with those of his creative collaborators. The director of the series, Glendyn Ivin, shares Lee's distaste for heroic representations of the Gallipoli campaign. Ivin's brother has recalled that his family "have never been all that involved with Anzac Day … I know my brother and I don't feel that identity and spirit that is said to have shaped the nation. Yet the horror of war, its stupid waste and emotional destruction is not something we take for nothing".[21]

Lee's script appealed to the show's leading actor, Kodi Smit-McPhee, precisely because it was subversive: "The story itself is very truthful, it's not so much chest pounding and patriotic, it's more showing the real emotional side and taking the mask off the soldier and looking at them in the most tragic times when they're terrified".[22] Born in 1996, Smit-McPhee was exposed first-hand to the cultural

---

19 Interview with Christopher Lee, 'Arts on the AU', www.theaureview.com/arts/books/author-christopher-lee-talks-about-his-new-novel-seasons-of-war, accessed 9 November 2015.

20 Author email correspondence with Christopher Lee.

21 Leigh Ivin, 'Gallipoli: A Defining Moment of TV Drama', 10 February 2015, www.northerndailyleader.com.au/story/2883068/gallipoli-a-defining-moment-of-tv-drama/, accessed 17 November 2015.

22 Andrew Fenton, 'Nine's Gallipoli TV Series Filmed its Ceasefire Scene with Real-life Gunfire in the Background', news.com.au, www.news.com.au/entertainment/tv/nines-gallipoli-tv-series-filmed-its-ceasefire-scene-with-reallife-gunfire-in-the-background/news-story/3947bc88cc11a072ae20bb548378d260, accessed 18 November 2015.

ubiquity of a resurgent Anzac legend that was particularly pervasive among the young: "We all know about Gallipoli and we celebrate the Anzacs but there's a whole side to it that was what we were taught in school but it was kind of just left because it was so tragic and horrible", he said.[23]

Harry Greenwood, who played Tolly Johnson's (Smit-McPhee's) older brother Bevan, also professed a hope that the series would encourage people to think more critically about the Anzac legend:

> [R]ight from the beginning we wanted to create this very personal and human re-telling of the story of the ANZAC soldiers at Gallipoli as it's important to remember that it was essentially a very sad, sad event. There was no glory and there is no celebration; for them it was tough and they had to face it unflinchingly. To tell the story, 100 years on, and try and remember the horrors of war is hopefully a lesson to people and for those to remember that war is never a good thing and something we hope we never have to return to.[24]

The creative team succeeded in their endeavour to create an "anti-war work". *Gallipoli* is imbued with a quiet sense of tragedy. Smit-McPhee plays the principal character Tolly as a sensitive and taciturn boy, far from the larrikin digger of national folklore. Tolly's youth is a metaphor for the young Australian nation: "Australia is a boy in a man's body thrown into circumstances beyond its control".[25]

---

23 Peter Wilmoth, 'Kodi's War: Gallipoli', *Weekly Review*, 29 January 2015, www.theweeklyreview.com.au/meet/1831377-kodis-war-gallipoli/, accessed on 16 November 2015.

24 'Harry Greenwood, Gallipoli DVD Interview', girl.com.au, n.d., www.girl.com.au/harry-greenwood-gallipoli-dvd-interview.htm, accessed 13 November 2015.

25 Andrew Fenton, 'Nine's Gallipoli TV Series Filmed its Ceasefire Scene with Real-life Gunfire in the Background', news.com.au, www.news.com.au/entertainment/tv/nines-gallipoli-tv-series-filmed-its-ceasefire-scene-with-reallife-gunfire-in-the-background/news-story/3947bc88cc11a072ae20bb54837 8d260, accessed 18 November 2015.

Tolly's sensitivity and intelligence allow him to act as a "camera … showing the audience the horrors of war".[26] And *Gallipoli* does not spare its viewers the horrors. Battles in which men die sudden and horrible deaths are realistically staged. Bloated, blackened corpses litter no-man's land. Exploding mortars splatter body parts. Some soldiers are eager to "get stuck in" to the Turks; others are troubled by the killing. All are burdened by flies, lice, poor diet, disease, heat and boredom. They are buoyed by letters and parcels from home and the companionship of their friends. Lee consistently veers away from caricature. The soldiers are neither heroes nor shivering wrecks, but ordinary men coping in extraordinary circumstances. The British commander, General Ian Hamilton, is not a conceited fool, but a decent man unable to rise to the challenge before him.

Channel Nine promoted *Gallipoli* in its typical bombastic and repetitive style in the weeks before its debut in early February. Nine's chief executive officer David Gyngell had reason to be optimistic: "Research panels across the country said *Gallipoli* was going to be the biggest show on television".[27] More than one million people tuned in for the first episode on 9 February, though perhaps the writing was on the wall when the show was beaten by Channel Seven's reality cooking show and ratings behemoth, *My Kitchen Rules*. That audience had dropped by nearly half the following week, when *Gallipoli* suffered the indignity of being beaten by Channel Ten's reality show *I'm a Celebrity … Get Me Out of Here*, and rated nineteenth in the top twenty shows for the week.[28] In its third week, the show shed a

26 Author email correspondence with Christopher Lee.

27 Annette Sharp, 'Gallipoli a Big Defeat for Channel Nine with David Gyngell calling it "Disappointment of the Year"', 27 February 2015, Daily Telegraph, www.dailytelegraph.com.au/entertainment/sydney-confidential/gallipoli-a-big-defeat-for-channel-9-with-david-gyngell-calling-it-disappointment-of-the-year/story-fni0cvc9-1227240605547, accessed 6 November 2015.

28 Craig Mathieson, 'Gallipoli's Ratings Fail Highlights Australia's Inferiority Complex', www.smh.com.au/entertainment/tv-and-radio/gallipolis-ratings-fail-

further 53,000 viewers, capturing an audience of 527,000 and finishing outside the top twenty programs for the week.[29] When the audience continued to fall away, Nine 'burned-off' the series, running double episodes.

The failure of *Gallipoli* to fulfil expectations shocked the television industry and became a story in itself. A journalist at *The Australian* thought the performance of the miniseries bore an "uncanny resemblance to the military campaign it graphically depicted. Great expectations were quickly followed by devastating setbacks and ultimately retreat", in the form of the "burn-off".[30] David Gyngell called it "my biggest disappointment of the year".[31] Commercial channels second guessed their Anzac Day broadcasting plans amid fears they might have over-estimated public interest. Reports claimed that Seven and Nine reneged on plans to send their morning televisions stars Sam Armytage and Karl Stefanovic to Gallipoli.[32]

Various reasons were advanced for *Gallipoli's* poor showing, both by journalists and viewers who contributed comments to online sites.[33] Journalist Craig Mathieson thought the failure was depressing evidence of Australia's enduring cultural cringe: "One of *Gallipoli's* story strands is how the Australian military was a misused tool of wasteful British generals, and while we bowed down to the British a century ago our empire of choice now is American. *Gallipoli's* falling ratings tells us that Australia's sense of cultural inferiority is as strong as ever".[34] Some claimed the starting time of 9pm was too late, especially

highlights-australias-inferiority-complex-20150218-13hwz8.html, accessed 2 November 2015.

29 Sharp, op cit.

30 Justin Burke, op cit.

31 Sharp, op cit.

32 Hornery, op cit.

33 For an excellent summary of social media commentary, see Jo Hawkins, www.historypunk.com/2015/03/my-kitchner-rules-why-arent-australians.html, accessed 19 November 2015.

34 Mathieson, op cit.

given the first episode went for two hours. Scores of readers of Sydney's tabloid *Daily Telegraph* decried the barrage of advertisements:

I gave up … too many ads.
Robert

I gave it a go but after 10–15 mins I was so sick of the ads.
John

Love the show with great acting and cinematography BUT
as always they totally and utterly killed the whole series with
[their] ads and [their] thirst for cash in with the series. It
was that bad [that] what I ended up watching was Channel 9
advertisements with brief moments of *Gallipoli*.[35]
Greg

Jaded viewers flagged their intention to purchase the DVD of the series in order to avoid the barrage of advertising. The experience of Albert, who described himself as an "unimpressed *Gallipoli* watcher" was evidence of the challenge faced by free-to-air commercial channels:

right at the time you are beginning to get into the storyline …
someone comes into your room and switches off your TV and
brings in dancing bears and a few snake oil salesmen to entice
you to do or buy a host of things that were NOT on your mind
seconds before. They all leave after 5 minutes and your TV
comes back on. Repeat this every 5 mins and you will soon be
cranky …[36]
Albert

The majority of comments on media sites were posted by men and their principal criticism was the volume of advertising. An article

35 All quotes from Sharp, op cit.
36 Ibid.

about the *Gallipoli* series on the *Mamamia* website, which has a large readership of women aged 25–49, suggested that women responded to the show differently from men. There were fewer complaints about advertising and more reflections on the themes of the show. LG64 was "sick of the jingoism and nationalism being shoved down my throat at the moment, I'm Team Australia'd out". Several women found the themes "too sad, too violent. We get enough of that these days …" Laura Palmer could not "sit there, week after week, crying through a TV show. It looks fantastic, but I can't do it to myself, not after all the things I have seen already and read about WWI. It's too horrific". Susan felt like "I've reached my tragedy quota. I can't bring myself to watch, I just don't have it in me". Chriswalk was among the majority of Australian viewers who preferred the more frivolous offerings of rival channels: "light drama and escapism, that's about all I can handle at the moment".[37]

Musing on the failure of *Gallipoli* to capture a large audience, a number of commentators concluded that Australians had reached "Gallipoli fatigue". Historian Clare Wright detected "a sense of ennui, almost a kind of nausea in a way where everybody is just over it. I don't think it's that there is a sense that they want to show disrespect towards the soldiers or the memory of the Anzacs but the way that that is being exploited presently".[38] Another historian, Jo Hawkins, argued that the official patronage of Anzac by governments over the past thirty years, through the provision of materials for school curricula and funding for museums, was turning people away: "I think people

---

37 'This Show Has Been Called a "Must-Watch" for all Australians. So Why Aren't We Watching?', *Mamamia*, 19 February 2015, www.mamamia.com.au/ entertainment/gallipoli-tv-show/, accessed 13 November 2015.

38 Clare Wright quoted in Alice Matthews and Nick Grimm, '"Gallipoli Fatigue" Causes Poor Ratings for World War I TV Shows as War Weary Australians Switch Off', *The World Today*, ABC Radio, 24 April 2015, www.abc.net.au/ news/2015-04-22/gallipoli-fatigue-poor-ratings-for-wwi-tv-shows/6413536, accessed 30 October 2015.

are at saturation point with the basic story".[39] Journalism academic Jason Sternberg claimed that "some people are fatigued by the story and that is compounded when they are presented with another TV show about roughly the same thing, Australia's national identity".[40] Comments on social media confirmed a sense of overkill. "We are quite simply Gallipolied out", declared lady_t.[41] Sam agreed: "From primary school onwards we are saturated with the Gallipoli story. It's a shame, but it's no wonder we are fatigued".[42] Albert thought that another re-telling of the Gallipoli story was "like trotting out Bob Hawke to talk current politics".[43]

The signs of saturation were compounded by the failure of other Anzac-themed shows. Channel Nine's *60 Minutes* Anzac special dragged the network's flagship show from its usual place in Sunday night's top twenty programs. The involvement of Sam Worthington in Foxtel's *Deadline Gallipoli* failed to attract viewers. Despite the fact that *Deadline Gallipoli* offered an original perspective on the campaign – something viewers claimed to want – it attracted just 76,000 viewers on its debut on Sunday 19 April, which placed it outside the top twenty programs on pay television. Quality did not inoculate against failure; the sequel on the following night was watched by just 46,000 people.[44] More congratulatory formulations of Anzac fared no better. Ben Roberts-Smith's valorisation of Victoria Cross winners saw ratings for Seven's *Sunday Night* magazine, which

39 Jo Hawkins quoted in Burke, op cit.

40 Jason Sternberg quoted in Australian Associated Press, 'Viewers "Fatigue" of Gallipoli Retellings', *Daily Mail*, 3 March 2015, http://www.dailymail.co.uk/wires/aap/article-2976812/Viewers-fatigue-Gallipoli-retellings.html, accessed 13 October 2015.

41 'This Show Has Been Called a "Must-Watch"', *Mamamia*.

42 Ibid.

43 Sharp, op cit.

44 'Gallipoli Fatigue?', *Crikey*, 21 April 2015, http://www.crikey.com.au/2015/04/21/media-briefs-gallipoli-fatigue-wsj-finally-gets-a-pulitzer-photoshop-of-horrors/?wpmp_switcher=mobile, accessed 7 November 2015.

routinely attracts around 850,000 viewers and occasionally breaks the one million barrier, dip substantially. The first episode, which aired on 12 April, drew 785,000 viewers, while the second episode a week later registered an audience of just 674,000.[45]

James Brown, a former soldier who has been highly critical of what he calls Australians' "obsession" with Anzac commemoration, expressed concern that public disinterest in Anzac television would be reflected in low attendances at Anzac Day services.[46] The concern was misplaced. Massive, record-breaking crowds attended Anzac Day dawn services around Australia. Attendance at the Australian War Memorial service greatly exceeded expectations, when an estimated 120,000 people turned out. Despite the rain in Melbourne and murmurings of a terrorist threat, there were more than 80,000 people.

The diagnosis of 'Gallipoli fatigue' did not match the symptoms. The public might have spurned Anzac-themed television, but its enthusiasm for the ritual enactment of dawn service commemoration had never been greater. Confounding observers even more was that the rejection of Anzac television was near universal. Audiences did not distinguish between sophisticated offerings such as *Gallipoli* and *Deadline Gallipoli*, Ben Roberts-Smith's celebratory documentary-drama *The Power of One*, or cynical tabloid productions like *Lost Stories of Anzac* – they turned their backs on all of them. How can we explain this?

The Anzac legend functions in the Australian national psyche as a cluster of lightly scrutinised but extremely powerful ideas. Faith in Anzac is buttressed by the twin pillars of Anzac Day commemoration and Peter Weir's 1981 film *Gallipoli*, and Australians feel little need to supplement their faith with knowledge. Many of those who

---

45 For ratings figures, see *TV Tonight*, http://www.tvtonight.com.au/, accessed 13 November 2015.

46 James Brown, *Anzac's Long Shadow: The Cost of Our National Obsession*, Black Inc., Melbourne, 2014. Views about Gallipoli fatigue quoted in Burke, op cit.

commented on the failure of the 2015 *Gallipoli* series referred to the film of the same name. A contributor to *Mamamia* noted that: "While Gallipoli is an historically important event, it's a story that's been told before and told well. For most people the movie pretty much covers it". Another commented that the "story has already been told so much better in Peter Weir's seminal film".[47]

It is remarkable that a film made thirty-five years ago retains such a hold on the Australian imagination. Weir's *Gallipoli* appeared when the Anzac tradition was believed to be in terminal decline. The conservative values that underpinned Anzac – loyalty to Empire and the notion of the superior fighting ability of the Australian soldiers – jarred with the progressive values of younger Australians. Overt hostility towards the Anzac legend emerged in the late 1950s, but it was the increasingly unpopular war in Vietnam that hastened its fall from favour.[48] The baby boomer generation came to believe that commemoration of war was indistinguishable from its glorification.[49] The brilliance of Weir's film was its capacity to recast Anzac in a form that appealed to sceptics.[50] In deference to the contemporary distaste for violence and blood-thirstiness, Weir and fellow scriptwriter David Williamson excised the film of violence. In recognition of the anti-British tone of Australian nationalism in the late 1970s and early 1980s, they turned up the volume on British incompetence. Such was the power of the film that *Gallipoli* transformed a tired tradition about war and empire into a potent myth of sacrifice and nationhood. The

47 'This Show Has Been Called a "Must-Watch"', *Mamamia*.

48 Carolyn Holbrook, *Anzac: The Unauthorised Biography*, New South, Sydney, 2014, pp.117–20.

49 Carolyn Holbrook, 'Protest or Propaganda? Psychology and Australian Memory of the Great War', Phillip Deery and Julie Kimber, eds, *Fighting Against War: Peace Activism in the Twentieth Century*, Leftbank Press, Melbourne, 2015, pp.291–312.

50 For more detail about the effect of the film Gallipoli, see Holbrook, *Anzac: The Unauthorised Biography*, pp.137–42.

film did not seek to glorify war, but by enveloping the experience of the Anzacs in an aura of beautiful tragedy, inadvertently, it did.

The film *Gallipoli* was followed in 1985 by a five-part television series called *Anzacs*, which traced the experience of a platoon within Victoria's 8th battalion from Gallipoli to the Western Front. The show's writer and director John Dixon had been trying to secure funding for his project since 1968 but was stonewalled by the un-popularity of the Anzac legend.[51] It was the stunning success of the film *Gallipoli* that loosened the purse strings of investors. Dixon and producer Geoff Burrowes were unabashed in their admiration for the Anzacs. In an introduction to the series, Burrowes told viewers that: "The story of the original Anzacs draws from the deepest well spring of the Australian national character. No story is more central to Australian national experience".[52] While the show was faithful to military events, it tended towards simplified characterisation. In an attempt to find a wide audience, Dixon resorted to an implausible love story between the show's leading man and an Australian nurse. He succeeded: *Anzacs* screened in 1985 to large audiences. A re-showing in 1987 also drew good ratings.[53]

Both Weir's film and Dixon's television series appeared at a time when Australians were receptive to a reconditioned Anzac legend. In retrospect we can see that Anzac was in the earliest stages of a monumental transition in the early 1980s and that Weir, in particular, masterfully seized the opportunity to remake the Anzac mythology. The version of Anzac pioneered by Weir allows Australians to mark their respect for 'the fallen' and to empathise with the suffering of

---

51 Daniel Reynaud, *Celluloid Anzacs: The Great War through Australian Cinema*, Australian Scholarly Publishing, Melbourne, 2007, p.205.

52 Geoff Burrowes, Introduction to first episode of *Anzacs*, quoted in Marzena Sokolowska-Paryz, *Reimagining the War Memorial, Reinterpreting the Great War: The Formats of British Commemorative Fiction*, Cambridge Scholars, Newcastle Upon Tyne, 2012, p.194.

53 Reynaud, op cit, p. 215.

the beautiful young men embodied by Mark Lee and Mel Gibson in *Gallipoli*. This version has congealed in the Australian imagination like fat over a lamb casserole, leaving Anzac impervious to criticism or suggestion. It is the form that is taught to Australians in school, preached by politicians and peddled by generously-funded institutions such as the Australian War Memorial. Tragedy, suffering and sacrifice are the keywords of contemporary Anzac commemoration.

Harry Greenwood, who played the character of Bevan Johnson in *Gallipoli*, is a pacifist who found grist for his belief in the series. By depicting Gallipoli in its brutality and horror, Greenwood hoped to inure Australians against the tendency to "mythologise and perhaps go away from the truth of what happened".[54] Such a hope seems poignant in retrospect. Yet, the failing of the 2015 *Gallipoli* series was not that it represented war in a truthful light. As with the rest of the Anzac programs of 2015, *Gallipoli*'s failure was its assumption that the popularity of the myth was indicative of a deeper interest. Like the religious worship to which it bears so many similarities, Anzac thrives on symbol and emotion, not close examination of 'what actually happened'. At the end of 2015, as at the beginning, Anzac rested comfortably at the apex of the national mythology. Its temple was sprawled across a distant Turkish beach-head and its scriptures sealed within the frames of a film called *Gallipoli*.

---

54 'Greenwood, Gallipoli DVD Interview'.

CHAPTER 5

Take One Sip When Someone Says 'Connection'

Passion versus Intimacy in The Bachelor/ette Australia

JODI MCALISTER

It is somewhat surprising, given the success of the American franchise, that it took so long for an Australian network to produce a home-grown version of *The Bachelor/ette*. The first Australian series aired in 2013, starring Tim Robards as the Bachelor. In 2014, the success of the second season, starring Blake Garvey, prompted Channel Ten to order not only a third season of *The Bachelor*, starring Sam Wood, but also the inaugural season of *The Bachelorette*, starring Samantha Frost, who won the second season of *The Bachelor* but was rejected by Garvey before the finale went to air. Since the inception of the Australian franchise – affectionately known as *Bachie* – a strong culture of online engagement has emerged. The most well-known examples of this are the recaps written for website MamaMia by Rosie Waterland, but recaps are also published by major newspapers like *The Daily Telegraph* and *The Sydney Morning Herald* and news sites such as Buzzfeed, news.com.au, and Pedestrian (as well as being written for the blog of digital publisher Momentum Moonlight by yours truly). Every episode is energetically live-tweeted by viewers under the hashtags #TheBachelorAU and #BacheloretteAU. For many viewers, it seems, a key part of the pleasure of engaging with *Bachie* is engaging with it critically.

Because of the nature of the format – one Bachie, many contestants – the show offers a proliferation of versions of love through its multiple potential romantic relationships. One version of love is ultimately successful, as the Bachie chooses a partner; however, this version of love is not necessarily the one most responded to by the audience. The culture of engagement that has emerged around *Bachie* is useful source material here, because it offers a useful litmus test as to which versions of love resonate most with viewers – which is very revealing as to how we think about, imagine, and construct love in twenty-first century Australia.

Love Languages: *Bachie* Buzzwords

Bachie is frequently lampooned for its distinct linguistic markers, phrases usually related to romantic attraction. These phrases are often incorporated into drinking games, which are apparently common pastimes among *Bachie* viewers, especially for premiere and finale episodes. Buzzfeed's drinking game for *The Bachelorette* (subtitled 'Get Maggoted to *The Bachelorette*') is a good example of this: it suggests that viewers should "take one sip when … someone says 'connection', 'felt a spark' or 'definite chemistry'" and two sips when "someone says 'journey'" or "'here for the right reasons'".[1]

Because these phrases are used – and overused – so much on *Bachie*, they have to an extent lost their meaning: a classic case of semantic satiation. That said, these words are revealing about the expectations of romantic love created by the show. If, as Niklas Luhmann suggests, love is a "symbolic code," one which "encourages one to have the appropriate feelings," these *Bachie* buzzwords are clearly part of it.[2] Understanding them tells us important things about the ways in which the show constructs romantic love.

---

1   Jenna Guillaume, Tahlia Pritchard, and Mat Whitehead, 'We Made A Drinking Game For "The Bachelorette" Australia,' *Buzzfeed*, September 23, 2015, accessed November 2, 2015.

2   Niklas Luhmann, *Love as Passion: The Codification of Intimacy*, Harvard University Press, 1986, pp.8–9.

Connection

The term 'connection' is (over)used in multiple different ways in the show, with references to 'instant connections' between Bachie and contestant sitting alongside the idea that a connection is something that has to grow and be actively nurtured (by the contestant rather than the Bachie, who presumably does not have the time to be looking after so many connections at once).

This, then, is drawing on multiple constructions of romantic love. The idea that a connection is instantaneous, based on something ineffable that passes between two people before they even speak, is not new: the mythology of Eros/Cupid and his arrows is an ancient one. But it is also one that is shaped heavily by a culture of romance. The idea of love at first sight is in play here, one that Eva Illouz suggests is a cultural label which provides a useful way of imbuing physiological attraction with meaning.[3] Although the idea of the 'connection' is not as strong as 'love at first sight', this instantaneous attraction is clearly still valued by *Bachie*, something we can see by the emphasis placed on the white rose. Typically, the Bachie will give red roses to the contestants s/he has chosen to continue on to the next episode. However, in the 2014 and 2015 seasons of *The Bachelor*, the Bachie has also had the opportunity in the first episode to hand out a white rose to the contestant to whom he feels the strongest connection. Because this is so early in the show, there has been little time for genuine emotional intimacy to evolve: instead, the white rose is given based on initial impressions only. Anthony Giddens writes that "[t]he 'first glance' [of romance] is a communicative gesture, an intuitive grasp of qualities of the other".[4] The prized white rose is based on this first

---

3   Eva Illouz, *Consuming the Romantic Utopia: Love and the Cultural Contradictions of Capitalism*, University of California Press, Berkeley and Los Angeles, 1997, p.4.
4   Anthony Giddens, *The Transformation of Intimacy: Sexuality, Love and Eroticism in Modern Societies*, Polity, Cambridge, 1992, p.40.

glance: on an instantaneous sense, based on very little, that a romance might develop.

This is not to say that the white rose is based *solely* on a glance. In the 2015 season of *The Bachelor*, Bachie Sam Wood awarded the white rose to contestant Heather Maltman, who ultimately finished fourth on the show. "I feel like she's someone I've known for a while already," Wood said in the first episode. "She's smart, she's funny, and she's incredibly beautiful, and I can already see the start of a connection there".[5] The phrase 'start of a connection' is telling. While the instantaneous connection is prized, it is not the whole of the thing. The connection is something that must be developed over time, through communication (which typically takes place, in the *Bachie* franchise, on the prized 'single dates'). This speaks to a modern romantic notion, which David Shumway terms "intimacy", as opposed to passion: "The discourse of intimacy makes emotional closeness, rather than passion, its Holy Grail," Shumway writes.[6] Passion – something which, we might assume, is at least partially inherent in the instantaneous connection – is irrational, immediate, and intense. Intimacy, on the other hand, is shaped by a deep emotional closeness which must be developed over time, mirroring the Bachie-contestant connection which must be developed.

Journey

'Journey' is perhaps the most frequently ridiculed of all the *Bachie* buzzwords (including, occasionally, by the contestants: on a post-*Bachelorette* finale interview on *The Project*, Bachie Sam Frost mentioned that she said the word 'beautiful' about a thousand times on the show, and laughed when host Carrie Bickmore quipped "at

---

5   *The Bachelor Australia*, Season 3, Episode 1, Channel 10 and Shine Australia, aired 29 July 2015.
6   David Shumway, *Modern Love: Romance, Intimacy and the Marriage Crisis*, New York University Press, New York and London, 2003, p. 3.

least it wasn't journey".[7]) But the ridicule levelled at the word has done nothing to quell its pervasiveness in the show, which signals its semantic importance.

The journey is one of Western literature's most common narrative staples, and it is one that is frequently interpolated into romantic stories. Even the most cursory glance at the publication guidelines of Harlequin Mills & Boon, the world's most well-known romance publisher, reveals the proliferation of the word 'journey': the guidelines to their Romance line emphasise the importance of the "journey to falling in love,"[8] while their guide to writing a synopsis describes the romance arc as a "journey from chemically charged first meeting to happy ending".[9] Romantic love thus becomes a kind of quest narrative: a journey from one emotional place to another.

For a quest to be a proper narrative, it must have obstacles: something which is argued by Denis de Rougemont, one of the first historians of love, who argues that obstacles are consistently generated in romantic narratives in order to drive the story forward, because without obstacles to overcome, there is no narrative.[10] The obstacles are clear in *Bachie*: on their quest for true love, the Bachie must overcome the temptations of false love and the lure of people they do not have a 'connection' with. Similarly, a plethora of obstacles are set before the contestants – sometimes quite literally, in the peculiar *Bachie* phenomenon known as 'group dates,' where contestants compete for the privilege of alone time with the Bachie.

In short, the idea of the 'journey' is a narrative one, and allows the show to frame the interactions of Bachie and contestants as a love story. It is fundamental to the way the final romance is constructed:

---

7   *The Project*, Channel 10 and Roving Enterprises, aired 23 October 2015.

8   'Harlequin Romance (Mills & Boon Romance) Guidelines,' Harlequin, n.d., accessed 2 November 2015.

9   Lesley Wainger, 'Writing the Dreaded Synopsis,' Harlequin, n.d., accessed 2 November 2015.

10 Denis De Rougemont, *Love in the Western World*, Princeton University Press, 1940.

as Jean-Claude Kaufmann puts it, "For someone who wants to be in a love story, the story is just as important as the love".[11] The journey posed by the *Bachie* process is foundational for the final romance: as Bachie Sam Wood tells winner Snezana Markoski when he declares his love to her, "When I think about this adventure that we've been on, I don't think of it as the end, I think of it as the beginning of what I know will be a beautiful fairy tale. But I also think it's important that we remember how it all started, on this crazy roller coaster".[12] The declaration of love marks the beginning of a fairy tale happily ever after – just as it might in one of Harlequin Mills & Boon's romance novels. But it is also the endpoint of a journey: a narrative of falling in love, of overcoming obstacles to achieve an ultimate aim. "To be in love is to be the protagonist of a story," Catherine Belsey writes.[13] This story is a quest story, a journey story, and such an understanding is intrinsic to the way we understand love in the Western world.

Constructing Romance

I have already referred to the work of David Shumway, who sees in modern romance a shift away from what he calls "romance" or "passion", which incorporates infatuation and attraction, towards intimacy, which privileges a deep knowing of the other: that is, communication and emotional closeness. In her monograph on romantic love in Britain, Claire Langhamer proposes something similar, arguing that:

> in the first half of the century 'to love' might mean to 'take care' of a partner, [whereas] in the second half of the century

---

11 Jean-Claude Kaufmann, *The Single Woman and the Fairytale Prince*, Polity, Cambridge, 2008, p.62.

12 *The Bachelor Australia*, Season 3, Episode 16, Channel 10 and Shine Australia, aired 17 September, 2015.

13 Catherine Belsey, *Desire: Love Stories in Western Culture*, Blackwell, Oxford, 1994, p.ix.

it increasingly meant understanding them and cultivating their self-development. Crucially it also meant expecting them to do the same for you. Psychic transformation as well as personal satisfaction lay at the heart of the new-style emotional intimacy.[14]

However, although the idea of intimacy is arguably the primary model in the modern West for romance, the idea of passion has not entirely disappeared. Indeed, Bachie Sam Wood's final speech to winner Snezana seems to speak directly to the excerpt from Langhamer above: "I've never felt like this about anyone in my life before. You make me a better man. I want to spoil you, and I want to look after you forever," he tells her, incorporating both the desire to take care of her and the idea that their love is crucial to his self-development.[15] Sam's love for Snezana, it seems, lives somewhere in the space between the two ideas of romance and passion.

This is not especially surprising, even though 'passion' is in some ways an old-fashioned notion. As Shumway notes, "[b]oth discourses promise a great deal in the name of love. Romance offers adventure, intense emotion, and the possibility of finding a perfect mate. Intimacy promises deep communication, friendship, and sharing that will last beyond the passion of new love".[16] While intimacy might dominate modern love more broadly, the format of *Bachie* places particular emphasis on passion and romance. Contestants have only a limited time with the Bachie, and much of it takes place in what we might call an adventurous setting: dates frequently involve extreme sports, such as skydiving or parasailing, mimicking the adventure inherent in the idea of passion. Intimacy is still important, and the show takes pains to demonstrate that conversation and communication between

---

14   Claire Langhamer, *The English in Love: The Intimate Story of an Emotional Revolution*, Oxford: Oxford University Press, 2013, p.38.

15   *The Bachelor Australia*, Season 3, Episode 16.

16   Shumway, 2003, p.27.

Bachie and contestant is key, but the emphasis placed on passion sets love on *Bachie* apart somewhat from what we might think of as "ordinary" love – if love can ever be said to be ordinary.

To consider the balance of passion and intimacy that must take place on the *Bachie* journey – these two different types of connections – I will now take one particular relationship (or 'journey', as perhaps I should say) as a case study. This is the relationship between Bachie Sam Wood and contestant Heather Maltman, who finished fourth on the third season of *The Bachelor.*

Heather, Sam, and the Problem of Lana

As mentioned above, Heather was an early frontrunner on *The Bachelor*, and was the recipient of the coveted white rose, signalling that Bachie Sam felt the strongest connection with her initially. Although this was based on only a few hours acquaintance, the reasons for this connection spoke directly to an idea of intimacy, because they were based in communication. "Our conversation is flowing so easily it's actually ridiculous," Heather comments to the camera. "I can't get over how much I can actually be myself around this guy".[17] Similarly, when Sam he gives her the white rose, he tells her, "Since I met you, a few short hours ago, I can't believe how easy you are to talk to".[18]

The ease with which Sam and Heather could communicate, and the speed with which they exchanged highly personal stories, was highlighted by the show, and well-received by viewers, many of whom believed Heather would be the ultimate winner. In the show's fourth episode, Sam and Heather went on their first single date. On this date, the intimate 'connection' between Sam and Heather was evident to many viewers, particularly after they had a conversation about her troubled upbringing and the death of his mother.

---

17 *The Bachelor Australia*, Season 3, Episode 1.
18 Ibid.

The news.com.au recap of the episode described this as "legitimately touching,"[19] while the PopSugar recap called it:

> actually the most heartfelt, genuine moment I can remember from all three seasons of *The Bachelor*. It's truly heartbreaking. This deep conversation sets their relationship at another pace and suddenly it seems like Heather's back in the lead.[20]

Rosie Waterland agreed, writing that, "He gives her a rose. They kiss and she is absolutely 100% going to win this whole Sparkly Hunger Games. Bachie Wood is clearly smitten, and she KNOWS it".[21] But this date also contained the kernels of what would ultimately be the downfall of Heather and Sam's relationship. "I feel like we're in danger of becoming fantastic friends," Sam confessed to Heather, clearly implying that, while the ease of their communication boded well for a relationship – mobilising an idea of intimacy – there might not be a romantic, passionate 'spark' between the two. Sam was not the only one to express this thought: "I can't see anything romantic between them," contestant Emily Simms remarked.[22]

Heather did not share Sam and Emily's feelings on this matter, repeatedly insisting that her feelings for Sam were more than friendship, while simultaneously stating that she believed a solid friendship was the foundation for a lasting romantic relationship. "I think before anything else, I want to find someone I can be friends with ... I just want you to be a mate that I could go have a beer with," she told Sam

---

19 Jo Thornely, 'Jo Thornely Recaps *The Bachelor* Episode 4: Where a Tiny Peck on the Mouth Can Mean the End of Civilisation as We Know It', news.com.au, 7 August 2015, accessed 2 November 2015.

20 Genevieve Rota, '10 Things You Need to Know About Episode 4 of *The Bachelor*', PopSugar, 9 August 2015, accessed 2 November 2015.

21 Rosie Waterland, 'Rosie Recaps Episode 4: It's Obvious in the First 5 Minutes which Girls are Going Tonight', MamaMia, 6 August 2015, accessed 2 November 2015.

22 *The Bachelor Australia*, Season 3, Episode 4, Channel 10 and Shine Australia, aired 6 August 2015.

on their first meeting: a notion that she stuck to through the entire series.[23] While Sam initially told her that he was open to this vision of friendship-first romance, as the series progressed, he changed his mind. "Every time I try to explore the romance with Heather, she bails out a little bit," Sam claimed in the thirteenth episode. "She'll go to calling me 'dude' or 'man' and it's really hard to go to that next romantic level".[24] The 'romance' Sam is referring to here is almost exactly the romance referred to by Shumway: a level of passion and intense emotion that is not based on communication, but on a sort of ineffable attraction.

The fact that Sam felt his connection with Heather was missing this passionate element became particularly evident – to viewers, and, one imagines, to him – after he met intruder and eventual series runner-up Lana Jeavons-Fellows in the ninth episode. Sam had an instantaneous attraction to Lana – "I've got this sense of déjà vu back to the very first night where I remember how instantly you can click with someone," he said.[25] While he also felt an instant connection with Heather (as the white rose proves), it quickly became clear that these were connections of different kinds. When Sam talked about Heather, it was usually in terms of how well they communicated: "The great connection I have with Heather just allows us to pick up where we left off – the banter's there, the jokes are there, the conversation picks up almost exactly where it finished last time," he said in the thirteenth episode.[26] When he discussed his relationship with Lana, however, it was in very different terms: "She has these amazing eyes, and I'm so attracted to her – I'm just not sure

23 *The Bachelor Australia*, Season 3, Episode 1.

24 *The Bachelor Australia*, Season 3, Episode 13, Channel 10 and Shine Australia, aired 9 September 2015.

25 *The Bachelor Australia*, Season 3, Episode 9, Channel 10 and Shine Australia, aired 26 August 2015.

26 *The Bachelor Australia*, Season 3, Episode 13.

how she feels about me," he said in the same episode.[27] We can see here clearly the ideas of passion and intimacy represented. With Heather, Sam had intimacy but not passion; with Lana, passion, but not necessarily intimacy.

The comparison between Heather and Lana was subtly encouraged by the show. Physically, they looked quite similar, and they were often dressed alike: for example, when Lana entered the show in the ninth episode, she wore a sparkly black dress almost identical to the one Heather wore in the first episode. This similarity was picked up quickly by recappers: Rosie Waterland immediately dubbed Lana "Heather 2.0"[28] while the *Daily Mail* ran an article about the pair's similarities, called 'Double Trouble'.[29] However, despite the visual similarities between the two, the differences in their romantic "connections" with Sam were also noticed. In her recap for the tenth episode, discussing Sam and Lana, Waterland wrote that:

> Bachie Wood insists that she's a really, *really* 'interesting' person, a strange adjective to use when he's only spoken to her for a total of fifteen minutes. But then, I suppose we do need to remember that Bachie Wood often confuses the word 'interesting' with 'hot', and then his Bachie Peen gets all kinds of confused.

In the same recap, discussing Sam and Heather, she wrote that:

> He gives her a rose. They kiss. Talk about feelings and she's clearly won this whole freaking thing unless he ends up loving

---

27 Ibid.

28 Rosie Waterland, 'Rosie Recaps The Bachelor Episode 9: Guess Which Girl Just Stormed Out during the Rose Ceremony?' MamaMia, 27 August 2015, accessed 2 November 2015.

29 'Double Trouble! *The Bachelor*'s Heather Maltman and Lana Jeavons-Fellows Show Sam Wood Has a Type with Their Similar Features and Identical Side-Part Hairstyles', *The Daily Mail*, 26 August 2015, accessed 2 November 2015.

her like a little sister or something except nah he won't she is clearly the one who will engulf his Bachie Peen for eternity.[30]

Sam's passionate connection with Lana is portrayed here as shallow compared to the intimate one he shares with Heather. But the introduction of Lana fundamentally changed the … journey? … for Heather and Sam. I do not presume to know here the emotions felt on either side, but in terms of the narrative presented by *The Bachelor*, there was a definite shift. Whereas previously, Heather had been identified by many as the frontrunner, the emergence of Lana provided a major plot twist in the love story. In her recap of a Sam/Lana date in the eleventh episode, Rosie Waterland wrote that:

> They dance, and Bachie Wood says that Lana has knocked his Bachie Peen sideways and talks about falling in love really fast and says something about 'reassessing where his heart is at' and oh holy Oprah this chick has won this whole damn thing. HOW COULD YOU FALL OUT OF LOVE WITH HEATHER THAT FAST? YOU LOVE HEATHER NOT LANA THIS ISN'T RIGHT.
>
> … He's mesmerised by her. He cannot even deal with his Bachie Peen tingles right now. He can't even remember Heather's *name* at this point. Heather is dead to him. He wants Lana to engulf his peen forever and ever.[31]

Lana thus became one of the new frontrunners, her passionate connection with Sam apparently trumping Heather's intimate one. In the fourteenth episode, where Heather was eliminated, it seems unlikely

30 Rosie Waterland, 'Rosie Recaps The Bachelor Episode 10: The Lights Went Out. Naughty Things Happened,' MamaMia, 28 August 2015, accessed 2 November 2015.
31 Rosie Waterland, 'Rosie Recaps The Bachelor Ep 11: Bachie Wood Finally Realised He Can't Keep All the Girls. Breaks Down', MamaMia, 3 September 2015, accessed 2 November 2015.

that it was an accident that Sam gave roses to fellow contestants Snezana and Sarah before climactically choosing between Lana and Heather: a symbolic choice between passion and intimacy. "I've been wanting and hoping that what I've felt has been an amazing friendship can become more, but I just don't think it can," Sam tells Heather.[32]

It is worth noting that Sam ultimately rejected Lana as well, choosing Snezana in the season finale, with whom, as I noted above, he shared a connection incorporating both intimacy and passion. But the disparate reactions to the eliminations of Heather and Lana signal something quite clear about the way viewers imagined romantic love. Heather was a fan favourite, but Lana was not. On Lana's elimination, viewers were largely relieved. Arguably, this had more to do with the fact that winner Snezana (affectionately dubbed "Parmie") was well-liked, but on the whole, audiences never warmed to Lana. Heather's elimination, on the other hand, led to an outpouring on social media. 2Day FM wrote that the episode in which she was eliminated was "epically mindblowing [and] life-altering" and "the nation has been in shock since",[33] while news.com.au ran an article entitled 'Sam Wood slammed after dumping Heather on *The Bachelor*'.[34] Similar articles were run by many other news sites. PopSugar published a piece called 'Why Heather Ticks All the Girlfriend Boxes,' demonstrating just how strongly viewers had espoused the idea that Heather – and the idea of intimacy her connection with Sam represented – was ideal.[35] (I, I must confess, added my own voice to this trend of pro-Heather thinkpieces – my recap of the episode in which she was eliminated was

---

32 *The Bachelor Australia*, Season 3, Episode 14, Channel 10 and Shine Australia, aired 10 September 2015.

33 'Bachelor's Sam and Heather No Longer Friends?' 2DayFM, September 11, 2015, accessed 2 November 2015.

34 Tiffany Dunk, 'Sam Wood Slammed After Dumping Heather on *The Bachelor*', news.com.au, 11 September 2015, accessed 2 November 2015.

35 Genevieve Rota, 'One Guy's Opinion: Why Heather Ticks All the Girlfriend Boxes', PopSugar, September 15, 2015, accessed November 2, 2015.

liberally filled with "true love" gifs from *The Princess Bride*.)[36] What was particularly telling was the enormous groundswell of support for Heather to take on the mantle of Bachie in the 2016 season of *The Bachelorette*: to begin a new narrative journey explicitly positioned as heroine of a romance. This demonstrates clearly how her particular style of doing romance, based on conversation, jokes, and friendship, resonated strongly with the viewership.

Bachie and, in particular, the responses to it, is fruitful ground for studying the way we think about and imagine love in Australian culture. While the show privileges the idea of passion, and promotes its importance in creating a romantic bond, the case of Heather shows that, on the whole, it is the idea of an intimate romantic connection that resonates most with Australian viewers.

---

36 Jodi McAlister, '*The Bachelor Australia* Recap – Season 3, Episode 14', Momentum Moonlight, 11 September 2015, accessed 2 November 2015.

CHAPTER 6

'Gaps in the National Family Album'

Australian Documentaries on the ABC and SBS

JEANNINE BAKER

During 2015 the main SBS channel (SBS One) broadcast just two commissioned Australian one-off documentaries (that is, not part of a series), neatly bookending the year: *Prison Songs* in January and *Black Panther Woman* in November. Although both public broadcasters have reduced their support for one-off Australian documentaries in recent years, many of those that have recently reached our small screens demonstrate just how compelling and important this art form can be in interrogating what it means to be Australian. This essay examines the decline of the one-off Australian documentary on our small screens in the context of audience fragmentation across multiplying viewing platforms, and changes to the funding and commissioning landscape.

The musical documentary *Prison Songs* (ABC1, 4 January 2015) features the inmates at Berrimah Correctional Centre, the largest prison in the Northern Territory. More than 80 percent of inmates are Indigenous, and the statistical likelihood of recidivism is high. West Australian director Kelrick Martin set out to make a film that went beyond the stereotypical representation of Indigenous people as victims. Martin told me that he'd had two major hurdles to overcome – "that this is an indigenous story, and one that involves inmates. I needed to make the stories penetrate, to push through the disinterest of audiences". The unusual level of intimacy with both the place and the prisoners, and the trust built up over a relatively long period of development and production, shows in the film. The inspiration was the acclaimed musical documentaries set in British prisons, *Feltham Sings* (2002) and *Songbirds* (2005), both directed by Brian Hill (who was a consultant on *Prison Songs*). Interviews with selected inmates are interspersed with songs sung by the inmates in a variety of musical styles, with lyrics based on the interviewees' own words and subject to their final approval. Written by Casey Bennetto of *Keating: The Musical* fame and Indigenous singer-songwriter Shellie Morris, the songs are one of the real surprises and pleasures of the film. The opening number describes the dehumanising, de-individualising effects of prison, and the numbing sameness of daily life inside. Sung by the main character, Max, the song also reflects the fear and humiliation felt by many inmates, and the lurking threat of violence:

Head down low to hide your shame
Speak up once when they call your name
Ticking off the calendar, doing it hard
Never let yourself get caught off guard
Start off scared and you end up scarred

There is no glossing over the crimes that landed these inmates in jail. But in allowing each of the interviewees to reflect on their life outside the prison walls – on their family and upbringing, and on the circumstances and impact of their crime, viewers are forced to consider the individual and shared experiences that led to their incarceration. Common themes emerge – family violence, substance abuse, and disconnection from culture and country.

Max, aged 27, is well-educated, articulate and self-aware, and probably the interviewee that most viewers will be able to connect with. "Anybody could end up in a place like this", he says. "Life's all about timing. It's all about circumstance". Max is "an example of the precariousness of life", says Martin. "One bad decision, one uncontrollable emotional reaction can change the course of your life.

Anyone's life".[1] The son of an Aboriginal mother and non-Indigenous father, Max did not feel fully accepted by either the mainstream non-Indigenous community or the Aboriginal community.

Dale, also 27 and light-skinned, says that one of the only places he feels like he belongs is in prison. Dale's story was the one I found most affecting. With eyes averted, he talks about seeing his schizophrenic stepfather beat up his pregnant mother, when Dale was just seven. That was the first time he'd ever seen someone hit, but since then he's witnessed a lot of domestic violence in other families. And when Dale drinks, he says, "the anger he holds comes out". The song that follows includes the heartbreaking line, "that's what you learn from your Mum and Dad". Max and Dale also rap together on a hip hop song for "all the outcasts".

Phil, aged 53, has become institutionalised, but says that the place he dubs the "Berrimah Hilton" has saved him. "When I get out I miss this dirty place. I know when I'm in here I'm straight, I've got my health back, I'm alive, I feel alive. I'm not out on the streets mixed up in crime". Like other interviewees, Phil grew up witnessing a lot of family violence.

The longing for home, family and the bush is palpable. Occasional glimpses of landscape, sky, and birds overhead are interspersed with images of the bareness of the prisoners' surroundings and the barbed wire that hems them in. Prison life "is sad and lonely", says Wurdankardi, 51, from Wadeye. "All I think about is my mother country. It's over there. Not here. This place is no good". Wurdankardi talks about the issue of having two laws operating within one nation, which has resulted in many Aboriginal people being punished twice for the same crime, and in what he sees as a lack of understanding

---

1 Victoria Laurie, 'SBS documentary Prison Songs tells inmates' tales in their own words', *The Australian*, 1 January 2015, www.theaustralian.com.au/arts/television/sbs-documentary-prison-songs-tells-inmates-tales-in-their-own-words/story-fn9d34el-1227171288538.

of Aboriginal ways. "Your story is down there somewhere, and the whitefella's story sits on top of it".

The lack of narration is refreshing, when much factual television is irritatingly over-narrated. Instead, facts and figures are conveyed by occasional superimpositions. One reveals that 90 percent of inmates have been involved in or witnessed domestic violence, another that most inmates committed their crimes under the influences of drugs or alcohol. Malcolm, aged 20, sings a song about his "precious love", which turns out to be alcohol. Despite its serious message, the musical number is upbeat and entertaining, and includes a routine in which female inmates dance with mops, reminiscent of Gene Kelly's famed 1943 routine in 'Let Me Call You Sweetheart'. Director Kelrick Martin, who grew up in Broome as a fan of Jimmy Chi and shows like *Bran Nue Dae*, cleverly uses humour and music as a means of "subverting the message and twisting perceptions". There is the glimmer of hope, as Max and Dale talk about the future. Dale wants "to change, break the cycle, start a family, do something for my people. But it's hard, hard to do that. I need to be able to help myself to help others".

The baffling decision to screen the documentary at 9.30pm Sunday night, in early January, meant that despite uniformly positive media coverage *Prison Songs* failed to reach the audience it richly deserved. Ground-breaking in its style and content, *Prison Songs* was also unusual simply because it was a one-off Australian television documentary, at a time when this kind of program is being overtaken by the documentary series. I am not arguing that series are not deserving of support – they are. During 2015, Australian programs such as *Go Back to Where You Came From* (now in its third season) on SBS and *Changing Minds: The Inside Story* on the ABC used the series format effectively, to draw in audiences and interrogate complex contemporary issues. But the dramatic decline in the one-off television documentary is worth close examination.

The Head of Documentaries at SBS, John Godfrey, had high hopes that the combination of a provocative subject and an experienced director (Rachel Perkins) would translate to good ratings for *Black Panther Woman* (SBS One, 1 November).[2] It is the story of Sydney musician and singer Marlene Cummins, one of the key members of the Brisbane chapter of the Black Panthers, founded in December 1971 by the charismatic and fiery Denis Walker. In the opening sequence Cummins' words signal that the film is going to touch on some difficult subjects: "Things were so bad for blackfellas back then. We were angry, in your face, but we were so young. Us women were on the frontline too. Some of us, we paid a price". Cummins reflects on her experiences in the short-lived Panthers (the group lasted less than a year), and her troubled relationship with Walker. We follow her to New York University where she addresses a conference attended by representatives of the worldwide Black Panther movement.

The role of women within the Aboriginal civil rights movements of the late 1960s and 1970s has previously been under-explored on television. Of particular interest is the relationship between female Aboriginal activists and those in the broader feminist movement. American academic and former Black Panther Kathleen Cleaver explains in the film that the female liberationists "were assuming that their pattern was our pattern [and said] that women have to be liberated from powerful men. But what we needed to be liberated from was racism". Aboriginal activist Isabel Coe argued at the time that they couldn't afford to "split the movement". I would have liked to hear more about these ripples of influence, and about how the Australian groups differentiated from the US Black Panthers, for example in the Australians' focus on land rights. Crucially, as with Darlene Johnson's

---

2   Phone conversation with John Godfrey, 29 October 2015; SBS figures show that the consolidated audience for *Black Panther Woman* was 105,000 (95,000 initial broadcast, and 10,000 time-shifted), just 2.6 percent of the metropolitan audience share. Despite several requests, ABC Factual declined to be interviewed for this essay.

documentary about the beginnings of the National Black Theatre, *The Redfern Story* (2014), this is a story told entirely from an Indigenous perspective.

The film also details Cummins' lengthy battles with substance abuse and gambling, her description of Walker's violent behaviour towards women, and her allegations of sexual abuse by two unnamed Indigenous elders. Making these serious allegations public was a courageous decision. The personal narrative style of the film, however, makes it hard to incorporate (or even acknowledge) alternative or contradictory viewpoints. An end card states simply that Walker disputes Cummins' account of their relationship. The damaging implication is that the Australian Black Power movement cultivated a widespread culture of sexual violence. "I think it's time black women of this country came out with the truth of the abuses. Without witch hunting, without necessarily demonising black men either", says Cummins in the film. But the broader issues relating to the relationship between masculinity, violence and the Aboriginal rights movement are not explored. This remains Cummins' personal story, and there are no voices of other Aboriginal women activists to add weight to her claims.

In past years SBS TV, through the activities of its separate commissioning arm SBS Independent (SBSi), which was established in 1994, built a strong reputation for supporting one-off and "typically highly idiosyncratic" Australian documentaries. These were broadcast within slots and strands that encouraged audiences to expect diversity of style and content.[3] After SBSi was merged with the main channel in

---

3   Trish FitzSimons, Pat Laughren and Dugald Williamson, *Australian Documentary: History, Practices and Genres*, Cambridge University Press, Melbourne, 2011, p.175.

2007, the number of one-off commissioned Australian documentaries began to decline. Commissioned documentaries involve a substantial commitment of funds for production (typically over $150,000), under a presale agreement that licenses the completed film for a limited number of broadcasts. All commissioned documentaries, Godfrey stresses, must fit the SBS Charter and "explore multicultural Australia". The SBS website states that commissioning decisions are based on four "key values": "To provoke debate, push boundaries, surprise audiences, and inspire change".

SBS screened five commissioned Australian documentary series in 2015. The clear ratings winner was *Struggle Street*, which garnered an extraordinary 23 percent of the metropolitan free-to-air (FTA) audience share when it was broadcast in May 2015, fuelled initially by a sometimes-heated public conversation about the merits of the series and its impact on the Western Sydney community that it profiled. The number of commissioned single Australian documentaries is due to rise in 2016, advises Godfrey, but in future they will need to be tied to a newsworthy event or to a larger theme, in order to create sustained media coverage and to "fight for an audience".

The idea that commissioning decisions are being made on the basis of marketing potential – rather than content, story and artistic measures – is deeply depressing to many independent documentary makers. SBS recently declined to acquire the documentary *Love Marriage in Kabul* (2014), directed by Amin Palangi and produced by Pat Fiske, despite clear pertinence to the SBS charter and its success on the international film festival circuit, arguing that it would not attract "a broad enough audience". The denial of an FTA broadcast is a blow for independent filmmakers on several fronts. Not only do they lose the potential to reach a large national audience, but also an income that could be used to repay debts incurred in the development, production and marketing of their films (it is common for independent filmmakers to partially or wholly finance their films themselves). They also miss out on royalties that apply when educational institutions copy broadcast material for classroom use.

As audiences fragment across multiplying viewing platforms, the increasing pressure on all free-to-air television channels to compete has resulted in a trend for 'event' programming that can attract publicity and hence a reasonable proportion of the shrinking mass audience. Occasionally, major documentaries such as *Hitting Home* are packaged and promoted as nationally important viewing events, but many one-off documentaries are not able to demand the same level of attention from the broadcaster's publicity department. Faced with successive budget cuts, public broadcasters have also been forced to compete and to justify their relevance (and their funding) to government. The ways Australian audiences are consuming screen content are changing rapidly, but television continues to attract the largest audiences of all platforms. The federal government's funding body Screen Australia has acknowledged that the typical style, content and format of many television documentaries has also evolved in recent years:

> Today's television schedules for documentary tend to include larger volumes of lighter factual programming and repeat series, alongside proportionally lower levels of more intensively researched or authorial documentary forms, all complemented by dedicated online content. However, technology has made it easier for audiences to engage beyond the television set, opening up opportunities to create alternative viewing options for specialized audiences.[4]

Since 1997, production of documentaries by independent production companies (rather than in-house by broadcasters) has been increasing steadily. Funding of documentary production comes primarily from

---

4   Screen Australia discussion paper, 'Documentary Funding: Stories That Matter', released 4 March 2014.

the broadcasters (mainly the ABC and SBS) and other industry sources, with Screen Australia funding comprising a minor part of overall documentary production. Although Screen Australia is still funding a great many single documentaries, they are not necessarily ending up on FTA television. According to Screen Australia, documentary series production has risen dramatically over this period while production of single documentaries has fallen. Of the 311 average hours of documentaries produced annually by production companies in 2012–13 to 2013–14, there were 239 hours of series (57 individual series titles) and 71 hours of single documentaries (79 titles). This trend in favour of series "reflects shifts in broadcaster commissioning strategies, rather than Screen Australia decisions". To obtain Screen Australia funding documentary producers must show evidence of broadcaster interest, or have an alternative strategy for getting their film into the market place. Many filmmakers of 'authored' or 'point of view' documentaries are choosing to make feature-length documentaries that are funded without a broadcaster attachment, and initially aimed at the film festival circuit and cinema-on-demand (such as Tugg), in the hope that a broadcaster will then acquire it for screening at a later date. Only a handful of Australian documentaries (just eight in 2014) are released in the cinema. A recent example of this pathway is Damon Gameau's feature documentary *That Sugar Film* (2014).

Australian content on commercial FTA television is regulated by the mandatory Australian Content Standard (ACS) and administered by the Australian Communications and Media Authority (ACMA). While Australian TV drama production benefits from content quotas across the free to air networks and subscription television, as well as regulatory measures that require them to invest in new Australian drama production, documentary production is more reliant on subsidy.

The ACS requires all commercial FTA television licensees to broadcast an annual minimum of 20 hours of first-release Australian documentaries, between 6 a.m. and midnight, of at least 30 minutes duration, on either the main channel or the digital channels. In 2014, the three commercial broadcasters (7, 9 and 10) screened less than 133 hours of first-release Australian documentary between them: just 21 minutes per day.[5] Many of these hours are devoted to long-running, easily digestible (and undeniably high rating) factual series, produced in-house by the commercial stations and usually broadcast in prime-time, such as *Border Security: Australia's Front Line* and *The Force: Behind the Line*, both on Seven. There is no requirement for the subscription television stations to contribute to Australian documentary production. These factors mean that the main Australian market for independent documentaries remains the two public broadcasters. In 2014, the ABC, SBS and NITV between them screened an average of 64 percent of all first-release documentary hours broadcast on FTA networks (including the main channels and their digital multi-channels).

The ACS defines a documentary as "a program that is a creative treatment of actuality other than a news, current affairs, sports coverage, magazine, infotainment or light entertainment program". It also acknowledges that the definitions can get blurry:

> Documentary and the other program types listed in the definition are all forms of factual programming. These program types are not always distinct. They are on a continuum, with movement over time as new styles of program emerge and others lose popularity. Within the documentary form itself there are various genres, such as the observational versus fully scripted form, and hybrids such as programs which combine re-enactments and interview. This

---

5   'Comparison of Compliance Results [2005–2014] – Metropolitan Commercial Television Networks', available on the ACMA website, www.acma.gov. au/Industry/Broadcast/Television/Australian-content/australian-content-compliance-results.

highlights some of the difficulties involved in attempting to define or characterise program types too tightly. As a result, the definition of a documentary is a term of art rather than a precise description.[6]

The Australian broadcast audience is increasingly fragmented, and documentaries, like other kinds of content, are thinly spread over rapidly multiplying platforms. In addition to the main FTA channels, documentaries are also screened on the subsidiary digital channels, as well as online-only platforms. SBS Online, for example, has produced sophisticated web-only interactive documentaries such as *Africa to Australia* and *Cronulla Riots*. Outgoing ABC Managing Director Mark Scott argues that there is "a hunger for Australian stories in all their guises", but acknowledges that funding local production of drama, documentary and narrative comedy remains "a persistent challenge", particularly as a result of cuts over time to the national broadcasters and funding bodies. This matters, argues Scott, because "the work of the Australian content industry in telling Australian stories underpins Australian identity, culture and society".[7] As global content flourishes it can overshadow local stories. Audience fragmentation has led broadcasters and filmmakers to look to digital technology for new ways to get programs to viewers.

The ABC hopes that its new dedicated online arts channel will attract viewers who are looking for less conventional programs. "Viewing habits are changing", acknowledges the Acting Head of Arts, Kath Earle, and documentaries that appear only on the online

---

6   'Documentary Guidelines: Interpretation of "Documentary" for the Australian Content Standard', Australian Broadcasting Authority, Sydney, 2004).

7   Mark Scott, 'The Future of the Australian Story', Brian Johns AO Lecture, Macquarie University, 15 September 2015.

arts channel "are not confined by the broadcasting schedule or by other traditional constraints such as duration".[8] The online channel also gives emerging filmmakers the opportunity to produce shorter or smaller-scale projects, thereby getting a toe in the industry. The Screen Australia-ABC initiative *Opening Shot* (now in its fourth round) is also aimed at providing an entry point to the industry, by funding up to six 30-minute one-off documentary films directed by filmmakers aged under 35 years, to be screened as a series in prime time on ABC 2. Filmmaking is a tough business that is only getting tougher, particularly for emerging practitioners and those from diverse backgrounds. In its final report before closing its doors (after its funding was cut), the not-for-profit media training organisation Metro Screen noted that most (56 to 68 percent) film-makers who make a professional feature film or documentary make only one.[9]

In September 2015 the ABC launched Artsville, a new annual series of six commissioned individual Australian documentaries. Artsville is the closest thing to the old documentary strands, albeit with a significantly shorter season. ABC Arts hopes that Artsville will pay off in the long run with increased audiences, once they become familiar with the Artsville "brand". *Deception by Design* (ABC 1, 29 September 2015) explores the links between art, nature, technology and warfare, through the story of the international development of military camouflage. I was fascinated to learn of British artist and naval officer Norman Wilkinson, who during World War Two came up with an innovative method called 'Dazzle' to confuse enemy submarines by painting the sides of ships with bold geometric patterns. Australian history is not neglected, including as the film does the story of such notable Australian *camoufleurs* as

---

8 Phone conversation with Kath Earle, 10 November 2015.

9 Metro Screen report, 'Emerging Visions, Career Pathways in the Australian Screen Production Industry', November 2015.

the artists Max Dupain, Joshua Smith, William Dobell and Frank Hinder. When Max Dupain was sent to the south-west Pacific to teach Australian troops about camouflage he struggled to convince the sceptical troops of the virtues of deception and that "it's not effeminate to hide", as the Australians were convinced that warfare was about being aggressive, manly and visible. Unfortunately the film relies too much on narration rather than allowing audiences to sometimes draw their own conclusions, but at least it is not as bloke-ily ocker in style as that of *Struggle Street*.

Another Artsville documentary, *Cast from the Storm* (ABC1, Tuesday 6 October 2015, 9.30 p.m.) looks at the work of an innovative theatre program in Western Sydney that helps teenage refugees and asylum seekers overcome trauma. As these young people share their "storm stories" (how and why they came to Australia) and eventually perform them on stage, we learn why some people are forced to risk their lives to seek asylum, and see how art can be harnessed to overcome trauma.

Hopefully the Artsville initiative will attract and build audiences seeking intelligent, thought-provoking Australian content. But inadequate publicity for documentaries is an ongoing issue. The limited number of 'slots' available for documentaries in the FTA schedule is also a problem. Filmmakers with a feature length documentary have to either edit it down to one hour, or face having their film screen at unsociable hours.

This was the choice faced by producer Rod Freedman and director Sophia Turkiewicz (now Scheding), who spent years making their powerful documentary *Once My Mother*, using their personal resources, before they were granted any production funding through Screen Australia. In the film, Turkiewicz investigates the reasons why her Polish mother abandoned her in an Adelaide orphanage, uncovers the truth behind her mother's wartime escape from a Siberian gulag, and ultimately confronts her own capacity for forgiveness.

Both public broadcasters knocked the film back for a presale. John Godfrey argued that SBS had "already done Poland" with an episode of *Who Do You Think You Are?* featuring actor Magda Szubanski. ABC commissioning editor for documentaries Phil Craig finally commissioned a one-hour version. The ABC subsequently agreed to broadcast the feature-length version (which had garnered numerous awards at Australian and international film festival awards, and enjoyed a successful theatrical release), but scheduled it at 10.15pm Sunday (26 October 2014). "We knew from this non-prime-time, graveyard timeslot, that the ABC would do little to promote the film. Prime-time shows are the only ones to get publicity, including from television reviewers", wrote Freedman.[10]

Why does the decrease in the single authored documentary on Australian television matter? "The one-off documentary is a unique cultural form that is appropriate for particular subjects and themes, and particular styles of production", says Sharon Connolly, the former head of Film Australia (and previously an independent filmmaker).[11] It suits highly personalised storytelling and certain kinds of stories, such as biographical profiles and explorations of specific historical events. It is a form that is manageable by solo producers, who are often committed to rigorous interrogation, intensive research and long development. However, as Connolly argues, "it is not a form that is well supported by the current Screen Australia and federal government policy settings, which are increasingly designed to fund businesses, not people and projects".[12] The reasons for these shifts are complex. In the last ten years, the system of financial support from

---

10 Don Groves, 'ABC rejects Once My Mother plea', if.com.au, 3 October 2014, http://if.com.au/2014/10/02/article/ABC-rejects-Once-My-Mother-plea/NYTCZXWDKO.html.

11 Phone conversations with Sharon Connolly, 19 September 2015, 19 November 2015.

12 See also Peter Hegedus, 'Australian Documentaries at a Crossroads', *Metro Magazine*, No.181 (Winter 2014), pp.94–99.

government for documentaries has been restructured, for example by the collapsing of three federal agencies (Film Australia, Film Finance Corporation and Australian Film Commission) into one, Screen Australia, formed in 2008. The agency's primary function, as defined in the Screen Australia Act, is to "support and promote the development of a highly creative, innovative and *commercially sustainable* Australian screen production industry".[13] Fulfilling this function, says Connolly, has led to the agency "orienting its subsidy toward growing larger, more diversified production companies and projects that can demonstrate pre-production market commitments, such as pre-sales from broadcasters and guarantees from theatrical distributors". This drive for commercially viable businesses has ramifications for small and solo producers, as director John Hughes remarks:

> Australian documentary production in recent years has
> been configured from a practice of independent filmmakers
> developing and producing works in an artisanal mode, like
> novelists, writers, independent scholars or painters, in favour
> of a rationalised 'creative economy' where consolidated,
> larger companies deliver factual programming as outsourced
> producers to television broadcasters.[14]

All four documentary series that screened on SBS during 2015 were produced by larger production companies rather than small producer-director teams, and three emanated from CJZ (Cordell Jigsaw Zapruder) which, according to its website, "produces more original prime-time series than any other production company in Australia".[15]

---

13 Screen Australia Act 2008 (my emphasis), via https://www.comlaw.gov.au/ Details/C2008A00012/Html/Text#param5.
14 John Hughes, 'After Indonesia Calling' (PhD thesis, Monash University, 2013), 136.
15 *Kebab Kings* and *Go Back to Where You Came From* were produced by CJZ, and *Uranium: Twisting the Dragon's Tail* by CJZ partner Genepool.

Many experienced documentary filmmakers feel that the commissioning editors have become more populist in their tastes, and more interventionist, making it almost impossible to sell traditional documentaries, particularly those with unpredictable storylines or that require a long time in development. "Documentary makers are usually risk-takers," said filmmaker Tom Murray, "but broadcasters are increasingly risk-averse – and this has flowed down to the filmmakers themselves, because they are forced into making programs they know will sell". Kath Earle agrees that budget cuts to the ABC have meant that "a certain freedom has been lost, and there is less room to fail". Critic Julie Rigg argues that "the difficulty of funding films has led to a significant dumbing down of free to air television, and a near disappearance of the high-quality, one-off documentaries which once found a proud place in Australian cinemas and on small screens".[16] Murray warns that the decline in support for one-off documentaries means that "we are degrading our national family album, our national narratives. Our capacity for reflecting on ourselves in screen form has been diminished".[17]

Some subjects are best suited to the one-hour format, says Freedman:

> But the broadcasters don't want these films because they don't
> rate, because they're too chancy. It's hard to measure the gaps
> in our history, our heritage. When we look back at the one-
> off documentaries that have been made over the last couple
> of decades – they are telling us our history. No one's going to
> access cooking shows in twenty years' time to give us a portrait
> of what we were like as a country.[18]

---

16   Julie Rigg, 'Film festival success of Once My Mother shows audiences crave
     intelligent films', ABC Arts Blog, 18 July 2014, http://www.abc.net.au/arts/blog/
     Julie-Rigg/Film-Festival-success-Once-My-Mother-shows-audiences-crave-
     intelligent-films/default.htm.

17   Conversation with Tom Murray, 21 October 2015.

18   Phone conversation with Rod Freedman, 9 November 2015.

Many of the acclaimed documentaries of the last twenty years, such as *Mrs Carey's Concert* (2010), *Contact* (2009), *Who Killed Dr Bogle and Mrs Chandler?* (2006), *Dhakiyarr vs the King* (2003), *My Mother India* (2001) and *Rats in the Ranks* (1996), are exactly the kind of research-intensive, carefully constructed, risk-taking films that independent filmmakers are now struggling to get funded and broadcast.

There is an audience for documentary – evidenced by the large and enthusiastic crowds who attend film festival screenings such as the popular annual Antenna Documentary Film Festival in Sydney. In a global multi-channel environment, attracting viewers to scheduled FTA television programs is undeniably getting harder. Getting independent Australian documentaries on the small screen requires more than public subsidy. It requires commitment by public broadcasters to this form of storytelling. The digital era presents challenges but it should also bring opportunities – to find new ways for both emerging and experienced filmmakers to make and exhibit complex and diverse Australian stories that reveal our past and inform our present. In this global multi-channel world, I believe there are still social and cultural imperatives to allow Australians to interrogate and reflect on our national identity – and documentary is one of the best ways to achieve this. The danger is that we might not appreciate what we have lost until it is too late.

CHAPTER 7

Neighbours, the Soap that Whitens

30 Years of Ramsay Street

DAVID NICHOLS

> It was about time to look at the average family … Then you
> start thinking about where they live, decide on the street, the
> people on either side, the conflict … and you gradually build
> until you get the whole structure. Obviously, it's incredibly
> complex.
> — Reg Watson, 1985[1]

In early 2015, the renowned weekday series *Neighbours* celebrated its
thirtieth anniversary, and the media paused for a moment to reflect
on what this show had given Australia and the world. Unsurprisingly,
nothing of great depth came forward: academe – and even serious
journalism, which will delve fascinatedly into the minutiae of Bronies
or trends in the 'twittersphere' – generally dismisses soap opera
as trite and transparent, as if that assessment is all that need be
known to comprehend something which captivates billions daily.
This chapter is a critical appraisal of Australia's *Neighbours,* which
for over thirty years has celebrated suburban community, however
much its audience may have changed (for all of this century and
probably longer, primarily British; for its first year, it was seen only
in Australia). The chapter seeks not only to clarify some common
criticisms of *Neighbours* and of soap overall, but also to establish a way
in which to write about soap on its own terms. It seeks to recognise

---

1   Reg Watson quoted in Andrew Ferrington, 'Life in an average street: following a
     great tradition', *Canberra Times,* 6 May 1985 p.27.

the problems inherent in criticism of this long-running, focused and open-ended narrative form; it discusses the way we might see *Neighbours* as a celebration of home, place and suburb, rather than the locus of story, character and drama

Soap opera is formulaic; in that sense it is like pop music and spectator sport, celebrated cultures similarly touching and engaging many, if not most. Each form generates a slew of subtexts, some operating within and some outside its own 'world'. The complexities of a program such as *Neighbours* which, apart from anything else generates 105 minutes of narrative most weeks of the year, cannot be denied.

If it is common to assume that soap opera's audience consumes it agog, accepting its obvious artificiality as reflecting reality, it could also be argued that many elite critics have little ability to identify the 'soap' aspects of 'quality' viewing, particularly when it's located within the early twenty-first century's golden age of television – *Mad Men, Game of Thrones, Homeland, House of Cards* and so on.

Writing about soap is additionally difficult because character development can be fractured, attenuated and obfuscatory. Characters are ciphers in many instances, or they may serve as such in one storyline, yet as key to another. Each episode of a soap is (generally) internally consistent, but time can transform scenarios and characters beyond recognition. The 32 pages Andrew Mercado dedicates to *Neighbours* in his book *Super Aussie Soaps* shows this well: Mercado is clearly frustrated by the difficulty in making a text-based synopsis of this shaggy dog epic, in which twists and turns are often more contingent on actor availability and the battle for ratings than story sense. But soaps don't deal in 'story sense', any more than our lives do, and a soap is as much an accompaniment to daily life – a parallel universe, perhaps – as it is conventional story.

Neighbours is a place-based soap; the one thing its core characters share is that they live in Ramsay Street, Erinsborough. Questions – ridiculous questions, in the main – of whether Ramsay Street properly 'represents' Australian life, particularly in its ethnic, gender-identity, sexual preference, age and standard of living varieties, have been asked for decades now.

What Makes *Neighbours*?

Strangely, since it is Grundy Productions' most continually successful product by far, well-known television commentator and analyst Albert Moran has little time for *Neighbours* in his recent overview of Reg Grundy's career, *TV Format Mogul*.[2] It was almost fifteen years into his television career – as game show host and then producer – before Grundy delved into the world of serial drama, with the hastily prepared and instantly (intentionally) controversial *Class of '74*. As ad-hoc as it may have been, *Class of '74* uses a range of tropes that served Grundys well throughout its drama production. The show, incidentally, was set in Waratah, a fictitious suburb apparently close to *Neighbours'* Erinsborough: in a delightful piece of intra-Grundys metanarrative, 'West Waratah' has often been mentioned. Numerous soap operas followed from the Grundys stable in the ten years before the company's star show runner Reg Watson – who had already created a suburban soap, the short-lived *Until Tomorrow*, for the company – formulated *Neighbours*.

As well as character 'types' *Neighbours* consolidated much of the Grundy organisation's previous soap work, not least the calculated creation of hot spot spaces to facilitate formal and informal interaction – a school corridor, a hospital, in or outside a café. Christine Geraghty, writing about soap convention in 1981, has summed up a version of this in the British context: "The locations in which gossip can easily take place are ... among the most frequently used sets in the serial – the pubs and corner shops ... In these public locations,

---

2   Albert Moran *TV Format Mogul: Reg Grundy's Transnational Career* Intellect, Bristol, 2013 p.xi

characters can appear and disappear, as required, in a way which seems quite natural."[3]

Watson, credited as the creator of *Neighbours* (and before it, a Grundy show which has certainly appealed to viewers and critics alike – *Prisoner*), had extensive experience as an actor and broadcaster in regional Queensland in the 1940s and 50s. He worked in British commercial television for two decades before returning to Australia in 1973. In the late 1980s or early 1990s he was interviewed on the set of *Crossroads*, a British soap he assisted in devising and producing. The unedited and unexplained footage from the interview, apparently to be used in a documentary on soap opera or perhaps marking the 1988 demise of *Crossroads* itself, is available on YouTube. Here Watson muses on the success of *Neighbours*, which had, soon after its launch in Britain, become extremely popular. "*Neighbours* was a very difficult concept" to promote to television executives, Watson explains, "because of the simplicity of it." It was counter, he says, to the current "stock approach" of the early 1980s, which he saw as "very phony".

> You see American soaps, they are so intense about their
> romances … and nobody enjoys anything anymore … I
> thought why don't we do it more or less as it really is – so we
> got a list of … nice normal people involved in very ordinary
> situations. One of the classic situations in *Neighbours* which I
> had tremendous argument about … the great, great moment
> which rated its head off … was when a schoolboy kissed a
> schoolgirl in the park …[4]

Watson is being disingenuous; the schoolboy in question was Scott Robinson, atypically a recently married 'boy', in his late teens. Similarly disingenuously Watson – by this time in his mid-60s – explains that he based the suburb of Erinsborough, where *Neighbours* is set, on

3   Christine Geraghty 'The Continuous Serial – a Definition' in Richard Dyer et al *Coronation Street*, British Film Institute, London 1981 p.10

4   www.youtube.com/watch?v=pbfhO7GrPi0.

his Queensland childhood. Watson was born in Brisbane in 1926, but he may be thinking more specifically of a suburb; the original 'Erinsborough' and surrounding suburbs in the credit sequences between 1986–91 depicted an image of the (unlabelled) streets of the Coorparoo, Greenslopes and Woolloongabba area from the Brisbane UBD. Its precursor *Until Tomorrow*, incidentally, had been set in the fictional Vale Street, in suburban Brisbane.[5]

In the Australian suburbs as Watson understands them, if you go to the beach and it rains, your neighbours will collect your washing from the line, fold it and even bring it inside – they know where you keep your key. Similarly, in the suburb of Watson's youth, if you were to go on holiday, locals would look after your pets and "you know the dog's going for a walk every day". His question was simple: "If these people exist, why can't we do a serial about it". That 'if' is searingly rhetorical; Watson did not go on to countenance the unlikelihood of suburban community relationships remaining in aspic since his childhood in Depression and wartime Queensland. On the show's twentieth anniversary he revised this utopian recollection to be about "Brisbane, twenty years ago" (that is, 1985 – not 1935) when "you knew almost everyone in your street and what a diverse, friendly lot they were!"[6]

At the time of the launch of *Neighbours*, Watson was already emphasising the 'normal' nature of the show. He told *Canberra Times* readers:

> When we first started talking about *Neighbours,* someone said 'There's no "heavy".
>
> The heavy, in fact, is life itself. Once you accept that, then you've got a tremendous springboard for every drama you can imagine.[7]

---

5   Andrew Mercado *Super Aussie Soaps: Behind the Scenes of Australia's Best Loved TV Shows* Pluto Press, North Melbourne 2004 p.83.

6   http://perfectblend.net/features/interview-watson.htm.

7   Watson quoted in Andrew Ferrington 'Life in an average street: following a great tradition.' *Canberra Times*, 6 May 1985 p.27.

There is no end in sight for *Neighbours*. Similarly no one actor dominates; there are, however, mainstays, the majority of them male. Stefan Dennis' business-minded criminal Paul Robinson appeared in the first episode – in a nappy coming back from a bucks' night, no less – but Dennis, and the character he made his own, were absent from the series from 1992 to 2004. Two older cast members, Ian Smith as Harold Bishop and Tom Oliver as Lou Carpenter, both began in the show a few years after its debut – in 1987 and 1988 respectively – but are now only infrequently seen, if at all. Ryan Moloney's rural misfit-turned-lawyer and family man 'Toadie' Rebecchi first appeared in 1995. Karl and Susan Kennedy, played by Alan Fletcher and Jackie Woodburne, are ostensibly the long-running 'parents' of the show (since 1994), a role consolidated by the 2015 opening credits, which see the two standing, arm in arm, in the sac of Ramsay Street before the viewer's eye is hoist into the sky for a view of the street layout, its radiant houses assembled around the central asphalt. But ongoing cast members, while important, only augment and anchor *Neighbours*' core.

Neighbours and Place

To move into Ramsay Street is to become a *Neighbours* element, and also – in most cases – to be matched with a local workplace as well as domicile. Many schoolteachers, café workers, and mechanics – along with other professionals across a wide range of social strata, including in 2015 Mayor of Erinsborough Paul Robinson – work close to the street, principally in the school, the hospital or at Lassiters, the least probable of the suburban workplaces represented in the show.

In 2005, Watson reminisced that early in its run *Neighbours* "inherited a complete exterior set from another drama and I revamped it and called it Lassiters." It was one of a range of changes, he claims, which "strengthened the serial".[8] Lassiters is a luxury hotel complex

---

8   http://perfectblend.net/features/interview-watson.htm.

based around a set built for *Holiday Island*, cancelled in 1982 after just over a year. It has since served as a focus for most (if not all) café and bar-related activity in *Neighbours*. That is, aside from Ramsay Street itself (usually only a meeting place in mornings and evenings, as characters leave for work or school, or return from them), the Lassiters venues host plot advancing conversation throughout each or any episode. Additionally, regular characters can work in the café or bar, the hotel or other aspects of Lassiters' hospitality functions.

Because its proponents and its detractors are so frequently eager to apply a rubric of (selected) 'reality' measures to soap, it is enticing for the commentator with no particular stake in either camp to indulge in contrasts between real and imaginary. But *Neighbours*, like all soaps, is an enclosed world where the true reality is the television industry and the measure of the show's authenticity lies not in connections to real suburbia, but to its own interior truth(s).

Watson made an appearance on *Neighbours* in 2015 to mark the thirtieth anniversary of the show: he played the winner of a trivia competition. This was a delightful, deft and clever touch: the million components of minor detail that go to make up the daily soap of *Neighbours* are the very essence of the program. Most ardent viewers typically view *Neighbours* on a range of levels. In 1981, Geraghty wrote that "all viewers/listeners do not have the same knowledge" of a soap opera's history "and events remembered vividly by some are unknown to others".[9] Additionally, while viewers may engage with storylines, they will often do so in an extremely critical way, based both on their feelings about actors and their extensive knowledge of character trajectories, prior plotlines and the show's 'world'. These are the proprietorial, 'trainspotter' fans who value the social, cultural and television industry ramifications of the program as much as they do the show's actions. This is where a soap fan's responses and reactions

---

9   Christine Geraghty 'The Continuous Serial – a Definition', in Richard Dyer et al
     Coronation Street British Film Institute, London, 1981, p.24.

to the world of their chosen soap(s) are so similar to a sport or pop fan; the 'world' extends beyond the song, or the game, into 'industry' or 'behind the scenes' narratives which connect to wider social issues.

Neighbours and Race

In 2011, the producer of the highly popular British crime show *Midsomer Murders*, Brian True-May, caused controversy when he decreed that ethnic minorities had no place in his fictional rural town: "it wouldn't be the English village with them. It just wouldn't work," he maintained.[10] The kindest interpretation of True-May's words are that *Midsomer Murders'* viewers are looking back to an earlier (pre-postwar migration) time, but also to an earlier form of drama. This works if you consider the suspension of belief already required to enjoy a show so often ridiculed for the preposterously high degree of crime within the gentle rural idyll of Midsomer.

Perhaps there are some who see *Neighbours'* 'whiteness' in a similar vein: a comfortable throwback to a kinder, less complicated period in Australian life (although the 1930s of Watson's childhood would surely not qualify as such). No *Neighbours* producer has come out with similar statements to True-May's; there remains, however, a strong perception that *Neighbours* has a more or less all-'white' cast.

Neighbours has always had ethnic difference as a featured component. One central character in the first year, Maria Ramsay, was given an Italian-Czech heritage and played by Dasha (now known as Dagmar) Blahova, whose Czech accent was evident. As mentioned above, the married Scott Robinson kissed a girl in the park in 1989; she was not *any* girl but one Poppy Skouros. Poppy's father Theo was an early example of a stereotype *Neighbours* (and earlier Grundy shows) regularly featured, the 'traditional', hot-headed ethnic father,

---

10   Quoted in Hannah Poole, 'Incest, blackmail, murder – but no minorities in Midsomer, please, we're English!', *The Guardian*, 16 March 2011.

baffled by 'modern' Australian ways and insistent that his daughter adhere to social propriety of the 'old country'. Three years later, Benito Alessi – an Australian-born man of Italian descent played by George Spartels, who is of Greek descent – had a similar role as an easily angered patriarch in conflict with what were presented as everyday 'Australian' mores; there were seven Alessis in all, most of them played by Anglo-Australians.

Some of *Neighbours*' fans – those sufficiently engaged with the program to contribute to online forums dedicated to its themes and stories – are keen to defend the show from accusations of unrealistic 'whitening'. Thus, 'Tracey C' in late 2011, who sees the value in pursuing conflict-focused 'ethnic' storylines in the show:

> The problem with these accusations of 'whiteness' is that they come from people who don't watch the show, and therefore don't get their facts straight - e.g. there are quite a few non-white faces among the extras now, and there have been some regular/recurrent/guest black, Asian, or half-Asian characters over the years.[11]

Continental European-derived characters have, as mentioned, always been a *Neighbours* staple; Asian characters are more rare and have been prone to comedy stereotyping. A Japanese businessman, Mr Udagawa, made visits to Ramsay Street three times in the show's first ten years, each time requiring the Robinson family to make a show of staunch respectability to maintain business ties with a character more at home in a Hal Porter short story than a 1980s television soap. The nadir of Asian representation in *Neighbours* to date, however, is notoriously the Lim family, who briefly lived at 22 Ramsay Street in 1993. The storyline in which the family were accused by busybody

---

11 'Tracey C', 4 Dec 2011, www.neighboursfans.com/forum/index.php/topic/35728-the-kapoors-spoilers/.

Julie Martin of eating her family's dog is still reviled by many of the show's fans as both tasteless and nonsensical.

A large number of guest actor storylines have explored cultural diversity since. A considered move towards redressing imbalance, but ultimately perhaps potential wasted, was the introduction of the Kapoor family to 24 Ramsay Street in 2011. Priya Kapoor was principal of Erinsborough High, her husband Ajay a local councillor and their daughter Rani a high school student. Within a year, Priya was killed by an explosion at the school after alienating herself from husband and daughter via a brief affair with Paul Robinson; Ajay and Rani were written out soon after. Sachin Joab, who played Ajay Kapoor, was quick to air his grievances against *Neighbours* for backing out of a commitment to a "multicultural" cast. He was particularly displeased that Ajay and Rani were "sent 'back to India'. It made no sense to me for Ajay and Rani to be sent back to India considering that both characters were born, educated and raised in Australia. I encouraged the head of the writing department at *Neighbours* to send us elsewhere, but they chose not to". Joab blamed a change in executive producer for the dispatch of the Kapoors, adding that "they've now brought in another all-Caucasian family and returned Ramsay Street to all-white characters."[12]

'Tracey C', quoted above, was of the opinion that racial tension was a valid topic for *Neighbours* to tackle:

> I still think that the show is too conservative in regards
> to multiculturalism ... I would love to see a Muslim or
> Aboriginal family in Ramsay Street – not because the
> show needs token non-white characters, but because

---

12 Daniel Kilkelly, 'Exclusive: 'Neighbours' Sachin Joab on 'low-key' exit, diversity on screen, more', *Digital Spy*, 10 August 2013, www.digitalspy.com.au/soaps/ s14/neighbours/interviews/a505631/neighbours-sachin-joab-on-low-key-exit-diversity-on-screen-more.html#~polAfiylW3Kfmx.

multiculturalism, its benefits and 'problems', are contemporary issues that need to be explored.[13]

This is arguably, however, where she is out of step with *Neighbours'* views on race. The program has habitually taken a 'colour blind' casting approach to non-Anglo Australian characters. Michelle Ang, a New Zealand-born actress of Malaysian Chinese descent, echoed the perception when she claimed that *Neighbours* "had a little bit of a stigma, they really got slammed for being completely white." Ang claimed her entrée into *Neighbours* in 2002 was an example of what is known as "colour blind casting"; she says she "felt quite lucky" as her character, Lori Lee, "had nothing to do with my ethnicity."[14]

The casting of non-Anglo-Australians in roles that make no reference to a character's origins appears to have begun with the 1988 casting of indigenous actor (and more recently, playwright/screenwriter and creator of *The Sapphires*) Tony Briggs as Pete Baxter, a bank teller and aspirant Olympic runner. One writer, reminiscing in consideration of the issue of racism in *Neighbours*, suggests that Baxter's "race never became an issue and was in fact never even mentioned".[15]

Close on a quarter of a century later, *Neighbours* featured another young indigenous man in its ranks: as indigenous, at least, as Pete Baxter, inasmuch as he was portrayed by an Aboriginal actor, with once again no acknowledgment of his ethnicity. Nate Kinski is played by Meyne Wyatt – who had a supporting role in *The Sapphires* – and is one of a series of young gay characters in the show. "We have a character currently who is gay, Nate, who is a returned Afghani war veteran," Woodburne told David Dale on the thirtieth anniversary of the show. "It's not a big coming-out story or anything, that's who

---

13 'Tracey C' 4 Dec 2011, www.neighboursfans.com/forum/index.php/topic/35728-the-kapoors-spoilers/.

14 Michelle Ang Interview: Tribe, Neighbours, Outrageous Fortune, Big Mommas & Norman Mao, https://youtu.be/BHRBV4VqKuM.

15 'Steve', 'Racism in Ramsay Street?' *Perfect Blend* website, http://perfectblend.net/comment/racism.htm.

he is. He is played by an indigenous actor, but that's not made a big deal of, either".[16] Here, the tolerant nature of *Neighbours* and Ramsay Street is arguably emphasised by simple acceptance of anyone and everyone, their ethnic backgrounds being of so little consequence as to be entirely uninteresting to all characters themselves, including the 'ethnic' individual in question.

However, Nate's arrival in Ramsay Street is almost provocative – insofar as the peculiar nature of his genealogy is concerned. His uncle, Alex Kinski, had briefly been married to Susan Kennedy. Long-term viewers would have recalled that of Alex's three children, Katya, Rachel and Zeke, the first was played by a Nepalese-born Dichen Lachman and the second and third by young actors of European extraction. The siblings' mother, never seen in the program, had the maiden name of Sangmu – possibly intended as a Korean name although it is more commonly used to denote the sports division of South Korea's armed forces (!).

Of course, one's uncle can be purely a relation by marriage and Nate may be in no way biologically connected to the Russian Kinskis or the Korean Sangmus. It is in the eye of the beholder whether such tortuous melting-pot dichotomies between actor ancestry and character family tree are important. The consideration of Ramsay Street residents' likely responses to such issues goes too far into the realm of speculation to be reasonable. It is similarly a matter for debate whether the casting of ethnically diverse actors in roles which ignore their 'difference' is a valid representation of a multicultural nation.

This is *Neighbours*' next challenge. The show proceeds extremely cautiously on all fronts, so as to embrace as wide an audience as possible. Unlike some other Australian soaps – *A Country Practice* springs to mind, but so too does a clumsy predecessor, *Glenview High* – it has never tried to be an 'issues' show. Yet its compulsion to align

---

16 David Dale, 'The Tribal Mind: Neighbours turns 30 and stamps its place in Aussie TV history', *The Age*, 8 March 2015.

all empathic characters with a range of 'normal' values is what shapes its world view. This 'normality' is only arguably white (it might better be described as 'middle class'). But it is the reason that casting *can* be colour blind, and why most straight viewers would have little trouble empathising with the gay characters, the most recent of which at time of writing is the popular, recently returned, character of Stephanie Scully (Carla Bonner).

However, what is perhaps more extraordinary is the expectation in certain quarters that a program such as *Neighbours* should be required to represent a 'realistic' proportion of non-Anglo-Australian residents in a 'typical' suburban cul-de-sac; does insistence on such diversity come close to tokenism? Joab is correct in his assessment that the Kapoor family was a trio of interesting characters, interconnecting with other residents of the street; but their 'Indian-ness' was barely touched on, at least until it framed their departure.

The cynical observer might simply conclude that the intricacies of representation of realism are too much (and in themselves too dull) to incorporate into standard soap opera storylines; that while *Neighbours* can (and does) include non-Anglo actors, non-Anglo storylines are largely outside its domain – and Julie Martin's tangle with the Lims is an object lesson in why such issues are better left untackled. This leads us to the key component to *Neighbours'* success; a marginal, but crucial, aspect of Watson's original conception.

No Through Road

The star of *Neighbours* is, in fact, the one constant, that dead end where all characters abide; indeed, one of the working titles for the program in 1984 was *No Through Road*.

We can only marvel at the peculiar blend of tradie, teacher, doctor and other profession calculated to maximise interaction with other characters across generations. Of course, the six homes we see – as is clear from their numbering, 26 to 32 – only constitute some of the street. Watson said in 2005 that when *Neighbours* began he "told everyone concerned with the serial that Ramsay Street was a long street,"[17] which it may be, but the show deals only with the occupants of six houses at the controllable and 'manageable', even *defensible*, end of a cul de sac. The street has come perilously close to death at times in the program; its loyal unofficial website *Perfect Blend* details at least two instances when, ironically given its 'soap' status, it has faced demolition for the sake of a supermarket project.

No drama reflects its contemporary society purely: all need mediation and critical viewing to be understood. *Neighbours* may be, for some, a comforting reflection of an earlier time. It would be inaccurate to suggest that it can be a source of escapism for anyone wishing to flee to a pre-multicultural Australia, however; if the show did ever play that role, it was neither deliberate nor overt. If anything, it is a celebration of community and egalitarianism, where collective values of fairness are imposed and difference is only skin-deep. Realism, as mentioned before, is not 'the point' of soap. But while it would be hard to pinpoint the most unrealistic element of the *Neighbours* world, its tolerance and the tendency towards bonhomie of so many characters, might well qualify.

The author wishes to thank Claire O'Meara and Andrew Spencer for suggestions made during the writing of this chapter.

17   http://perfectblend.net/features/interview-watson.htm.

Chapter 8

Not the Boy Next Door

Reconsidering Television in the Musical Miniseries

Liz Giuffre

Music-focused television has continued to be popular in Australia despite international trends. While MTV moved on to reality programming years ago, we've maintained our love of music videos via *Rage* and *SBS Pop Asia*, as well as developing our own forms like *RocKwiz*, now ten years on and counting. Documentary and music was also tackled with *Blood and Thunder* – the story of Alberts music. 2015 saw the first official Australian entry in Eurovision, an experiment deemed so successful that we've been invited back again in 2016. But the major music-TV event of the year was *Peter Allen: Not the Boy Next Door*, produced by Shine Australia, the makers of the ratings-winning musical miniseries *INXS: Never Tear Us Apart*. Revisiting Peter Allen's life was the aim of the program, but, interestingly, nostalgia for that life was induced in part through a featuring of iconic moments of Australian music television.

The morning after the first episode of *Peter Allen: Not the Boy Next Door* aired I rang Dad to ask if he'd watched it. "Yeah, some of it, but I thought it was a bit tacky … There was too much emphasis on sex", Dad said. Dad wasn't disapproving of a particular type of sex; he knew Peter had male and female partners, and that just was what it was. Dad's disapproval was more with the ratio of music-to-sex featured in the episode. Peter Allen was often described as a 'flamboyant' artist – literally, this was a reference to his energetic and sometimes acrobatic performance style that often involved dancing on top of his piano. But, of course, 'flamboyant' was also a euphemism for Allen's sexuality. Allen's personal life remained mostly personal, and save for his much-publicised marriage to Liza Minnelli, he rarely discussed it in the press. Since his death much has been made of Allen's relationships with men. Dramatisations like the musical *The Boy From Oz* have implied that Allen's relationships with women, and particularly his marriage to Minnelli, were just a preview to the main (homosexual) loves of his life. However, to suggest that Allen wore sex on his loud Hawaiian shirtsleeve in the same way Michael Hutchence wore it in his tight leather pants simply isn't true. Allen's personality was the greatest source of his music's appeal, and the genuineness of his relationships was, at the end of the day, not really any of his audiences' business. Allen was not a sexy star in the same way a rock star of today is – his appeal was in the self-deprecating and softly risqué humour that was part of his musical performance. He presented himself this way mostly because of his genre pedigree, growing up on a cabaret and vaudeville tradition and eventually drawing these styles into mainstream pop.

My dad's point about wanting a musical miniseries to be actually about *the music* is a valid one, and thankfully, by the second episode the producers agreed too. In the end Dad just wanted more about Allen's actual music – it was almost as if he didn't think the rest should be his business, or that of a Sunday night prime time audience. *Not the Boy Next Door* was based on the account of Peter Allen's life presented by biographer Stephen Maclean in the mid-1990s. It's the same source material that informed the Australian and then Broadway musical *The Boy From Oz*, but the television miniseries used music in a markedly different way to the stage production. The stage show worked as a jukebox musical, that is, a narrative built out of the lyrics of a central musician's most famous works. Often there's artistic licence taken with building this narrative. A famous example is *Mamma Mia*, which created a story that was completely apart from the Swedish foursome that provided the soundtrack. By the time Peter Allen made it to Broadway via Hugh Jackman, the story of a small-town Australian boy made good had been much exaggerated and smoothed over, with perhaps his best ever song, 'Tenterfield Saddler', left out because of fears that an American audience would not be interested in a small town and craftsman in outback Australia. When *Not the Boy Next Door* told the story of Peter Allen on television, it did use music, but in a different way. The aim was not to make him and his context larger than life, but rather to make a faithful and thoughtful recreation of key points in his musical history.

The Music Television Series' Use of Music

Not the Boy Next Door began by establishing Allen as a young outcast, then a young lover and rogue. Thankfully it ultimately turned away from personal dramatisation to focus on portraying him as a developing artist and gifted songwriter. It featured a suite of the best of Allen's original songs as well as iconic songs of the period, with only a very small amount of non-diegetic sound in the whole series. Interestingly, the musical performances of the actors portraying Judy Garland and Liza Minnelli were dubbed, with specialist vocalists performing for each singer as actors mimed along. It was a choice that created a strange dynamic – and an interesting contrast given that the actors playing young and older Peter Allen were allowed to do all their own vocal work. Somehow the character of Allen appeared more complete this way – while the detached vocals of Minnelli and Garland left the audience feeling slightly distant from them.

The first time we see the young Peter singing, he appears live in the local pub in Armidale. Ky Baldwin, who plays Allen as a child, both sings and acts the character, and he looks like a tiny figure behind a piano, wearing white adult-sized cricket boots to complete his Jerry Lee Lewis-like stage act. This draws the audience into the musical performance, and the young actor's vocal tone is refined as he enunciates the consonants on rock lyrics of the time like 'See You Later Alligator' and 'Awop-bop-a-loo-mop awop bam boom'. The performance conveys the young Allen's ambition, and perhaps even his awareness that he needs to "fake it till he makes it".

Later in the episode the young actor sings a song that was actually written by the adult Allen, 'Tenterfield Saddler'. Peter Allen wrote the song when he was 26 on a return trip to Australia from the US, and 'Saddler' was the true story of his father and grandfather. In the miniseries the song is sung by the child actor Baldwin, embodying the memory of the older Allen captured in the hit single. The scene becomes a duet with Joel Jackson (the actor who plays the adult Allen), who starts to sing as well, making the song a bridge for a 'then and now' telling of the rest of the Peter Allen musical story. It's a sweet moment with just enough poetic licence, allowing fans of the song to enjoy its performance, and those interested in the drama to see the young child's journey into adulthood.

Female musicians feature in *Not the Boy Next Door* in a different way to the male lead character. Judy Garland (Sigrid Thornton) and Liza Minnelli (Sara West) were important professional and personal figures in Allen's life, and the miniseries tries to show both of these relationships on and off stage. When Allen and Garland first meet, Allen is performing in Hong Kong and gets wind that Garland is in the audience. He concludes his show with a solo piano version of 'Over the Rainbow' as a tribute to her. We see him talk to the audience before the performance, introducing her and telling them (and her) of his genuine fandom, but she soon takes the introduction as a provocation to take over the set and perform 'Rainbow' herself. She takes the stage and the microphone, and the voice that is heard is a flawless impersonation of Garland. However, there is a mismatch between the sound and image, and it's pretty clear that the voice is dubbed rather than the actor, Thornton, singing. The vocalist,

Melanie Parry, does a faithful impersonation of the real Judy, but as a piece of music television it seems disjointed. We go from a type of artist's impression of the past to an attempt to Frankenstein together Garland as a character. Parry's very produced vocals and Thornton's less exaggerated images don't quite fit together. Thornton's adaptation of Garland's mannerisms and her development of the complexity of her character are dropped as she ascends into her swan song.

In contrast, when Jackson sings the opening lines of 'Over the Rainbow' as Allen, his voice is clear and well-pitched, particularly over the notorious octave jump that opens the tune. But he also sounds clearly nervous, timid. Jackson's voice shakes in a way that develops the story and character beautifully – we see him as a nervous looking Allen singing in front of his icon, Garland, and we also hear that uncertainty in his voice. Jackson's screen performance is affecting because it's not the same as Allen, even though clearly inspired by his style. His version of Allen is allowed to be an interpretation complete with new additions, while Thornton's Garland remains musically a strict imitation of the iconic Hollywood star.

A similar affect is created with the vocal dub over Sara West's depiction of Liza Minnelli. The scene begins with a young Minnelli due to appear at the London Palladium with a now relatively old and relatively sick Judy. Allen has just met Minnelli at this point (even though Garland has tried to set them up) and at first she is dismissive. She finally confides in him that she's terribly nervous about the performance, and he responds by saying, simply, "Don't worry, most of the audience will just be looking at your Mum". It's a perfect comment to break the tension and spark the kinship between Minnelli and Allen. However, when vocalist Angela Toohey sings 'The Gypsy in My Soul', while actor West mimes, it's a blistering sound but a break from the vulnerable version of Minnelli that West had been building visually. Just a few seconds before we had seen West play Liza as a young girl finding her feet before becoming the famous daughter / future wife / socialite, but when Toohey starts to sing all of sudden it seems that Minnelli has grown up and matured too quickly. Interestingly, the archival television footage of the actual London performance reveals that the real Minnelli was much more vocally timid than *Not the Boy Next Door* allows, so it's a shame that the development wasn't allowed to happen here as well. Perhaps it was the intention of the music television producers to depict Minnelli (and Garland) as a figure always detached from herself in public.

The Music Television Series' Use of Television

Not the Boy Next Door shows that television, as well as music, played an important role in Peter Allen's life. Allen rose to fame in a pre-internet era where 'big breaks' couldn't be gained by social media 'likes' or viral video campaigns; television performances brought him and his music to mass audiences. During the miniseries we see how the big steps in his career were taken with television, with several key performances and their contexts recreated to serve the musical narrative. This use of music television nostalgia within the music miniseries is an interesting approach, and was used again in the Ian 'Molly' Meldrum miniseries, *Molly* (Seven, 2016).

The first music and television moment that is recreated in *Not The Boy Next Door* appears early in the series as young Peter Woolnough travels from Armidale to Sydney to audition for *Australia's Amateur Hour*. It was his first taste of possible broadcast success, and first showbiz rejection. The program, which had begun as a radio talent quest in the 1940s, made it briefly to television in 1957–58, and is used in the story as a way to distract the young boy: Peter's mother lets him audition as a divert from his father's bad behaviour. The audition itself shows the young boy giving his best hip-shaking performance of 'Whole Lotta Shakin' Goin' On', interspersed with his own fantasy reaction of the judges' gushing praise. The actual response is far less positive, with the panel advising, "Sorry, son, but we don't think you're ready for Australia's Amateur Hour". The sequence is a bit corny, but as part of the story it sets up the important place that broadcasting would hold in Allen's career.

Around the same time we also see shots of the young Allen watching television on the lounge with his mum, Marion (Rebecca Gibney). Chad Morgan's 'Sheik from Scrubby Creek' is playing and the two laugh at its silliness – the exchange serving to deliberately emphasise the bond between the two characters and offer a nod towards Allen's identity as a fan as well as an artist. The song, released in 1952, had been in circulation for a few years before television started in Australia. While this sequence is something of a stretch in terms of the historical timeline, what's interesting is how television's influence on the young boy is depicted. Morgan's novelty song and its unusual delivery show Allen's love of humour in performance.

Another music television event recreated in *Not the Boy Next Door* was Allen's first appearance on *Bandstand* with Brian Henderson. We first see him developing The Allen Brothers act in preparation for the television show appearance, an act that was constructed for broadcast originally. The idea was to create a duo with a clean cut image and the idea of the 'brothers' was a fiction, but it worked well. Singer Chris Bell (Rob Mills) was paired with Allen by a manager who thought selling a 'family connection' would gain attention, while also allowing the two singers to develop. This piece in Peter Allen's biography is realised in the television miniseries as a montage, showing Allen and Bell establishing The Allen Brothers' look and sound while practising synchronised dance moves and harmonies. The sequences are brought together with sound and images of them singing the song 'Up, Up and Away', with the lyric used as a metaphor for a career on the rise. However, it's a metaphor that has a few historical inconsistencies, with the most obvious being that the song (which *was* performed by The Allen Brothers at some point) was released in 1967 while the audition itself would have taken place at least five years earlier.

Nonetheless the rehearsal montage shows Peter Allen becoming one of the Allen Brothers, as well as his first real chance to appeal directly to television via a discussion with *Bandstand* host Brian Henderson (Scott Sheridan). Later we see Henderson introducing Allen to Judy Stone (Kate Ryerson), Col Joye (William Wensley), Patsy Ann Noble (Chelsea Brown) and a very young Olivia Newton-John (Christie Whelan). The latter is particularly important, as Newton-John was the other prominent Australian of the era to really 'break' in the US. This section of the series breaks into another montage that features a series of photoshoots for the young musicians that, curiously, is tied together with a recording of Johnny O'Keefe's 'Wild One'. Given that O'Keefe was, by this stage, the host on rival music television programs like *Six O'Clock Rock* and *The Johnny O'Keefe Show*, the choice is strange (as is the absence of O'Keefe as a character himself – an important figure in Allen's life and development).

The Allen Brothers would again appear on *Bandstand* some years later after Peter and Liza married. The miniseries recreates an iconic music segment from the show that starts with Liza singing 'Everybody Loves My Baby'. We see The Allen Brothers and Brian Henderson talking backstage before the segment starts, then Minnelli enters the frame and takes over singing, to later be joined by Peter, then Chris. The original clip shows the three of them performing in black suits and smart ties, with Liza something of a novel guest for the brothers at home on the local music show. The miniseries draws this out more by cutting away from the show itself to reveal Allen's family watching at home in the lounge room, then cutting away from the shot as the song continues to play over a montage of Allen buying the newspaper the next day. As Liza's voice continues "everybody loves my baby ... nobody but me" we see a headline in the paper that applauds Minnelli's performances, and doesn't mention Allen at all.

Given that this original *Bandstand* clip has since been recirculated and re-released on DVD and YouTube, it makes sense that the producers would use it as part of their research for the story, but also reference it for a contemporary audience still interested in the time. Like recreating The Beatles' appearance on *The Ed Sullivan Show*, this was a key part of the story.

From here on in the series seems to show Allen returning home to Australia always for a local television appearance. Given that by then Allen's schedule would likely have allowed little opportunity for extensive live touring, even then a free-to-air television appearance would still have reached a much wider audience than concerts ever could have. Firstly we see Allen back after his break with Liza, now long haired and vising Australia as part of a reunion of the *Bandstand* family. Allen and his mother are seen watching the pre-recorded show on television, initially as Allen appears at the piano singing his new song 'Dixie'. Henderson enters and says to Allen "thanks for coming back for the *Bandstand* reunion", a time marker to the audience watching in 2015 and a reminder that Allen's time as a young performer (and *Bandstand*'s time as a forerunner) has moved on. The two do a brief interview, where on the 1970s *Bandstand* screen Allen tells Henderson that "America has been going great", while the shot then cuts back to Allen on the lounge with his Mum, Marion, at home saying, almost immediately instead, "it's terrible". On screen Allen says "sales are going great" while on the lounge he says "I've sold two records", a remark his mother scolds him for, particularly for having "lied on national TV". The shot of Allen on screen is shown in sepia tone and framed by the old screen's wooden top and large in built speakers, again showing the music television performance as something that was consumed domestically and with relative informality. Quickly, Allen replies, "I know, but if you're going to lie, lie big", a comment that sees both laugh at themselves, but perhaps also at the whole music television circus of the time.

Immediately following this musical performance sequence and lounge room commentary the shot returns back to the studio on television and Henderson says "Pete, you remember Olivia from the old days?" Here Newton-John joins Allen and Henderson on the screen, met by rousing applause from the studio audience. She looks to him and says "When are you going to write me a song, Peter?", then to the audience she says "he writes the most beautiful songs, don't you think?" It's a comment met with more applause from the studio audience, and at home Marion mocks, "Ooh, now the pressure's on!" Although this meeting isn't a piece of television history that is still readily available (indeed, this appears to have been mostly fictionalised), it sets up a stepping stone in Newton-John's career, as her international hit 'I Honestly Love You' was co-written by Allen and Jeff Barry.

The next music television appearance within the miniseries is Allen again returning home to Australia from overseas, again after time has passed and musical tastes seem to have changed. Here we see one of Allen's most famous appearances on rock and pop music television, *Countdown*, also faithfully recreated. The appearance was originally staged following another return trip from the States, with Allen now his own star rather than part of a bogus brothers' act or as Mr Minnelli. The clip shows Allen with another 'flamboyant' music figure, Molly Meldrum (Andy Ryan), meeting on screen just after he's arrived home and finished a press tour and shoot for his new album. Again, this appearance on television is framed in the miniseries by the home television set. We see the recreation of the *Countdown* moment shown as if it's on the old TV set, watched by Marion and Allen's sister Lynn (Elise McCann) sitting at home. They watch as Meldrum begins, all large hat and hand gestures speaking down the barrel of the camera. "His name is Peter Allen, you mustn't miss him", Meldrum says with typical mumbling enthusiasm, with the show's name glittering in gold writing behind Allen and Meldrum sitting on a studio couch. Allen plays with him, saying, "Don't stop Molly, I could listen to you all day", a quip that draws laughter from those in the studio and his family at home. Meldrum asks what Allen will play and he continues to be flippant, saying, "Oh, something quite conservative. You all [in the studio] look like a classical music crowd so maybe some Beethoven". With this Marion chimes in "God love you Peter Woolnough", while Lynn adds "He hasn't changed one bit, has he?" From here the shot is taken over as we see Peter's point of view from onstage in the television studio, launching into 'I Go to Rio' for the *Countdown* crowd. This is the first time there's obvious dubbing for the musical performance (although the original *Countdown* piece was most likely dubbed by Allen himself, too). Unlike the pieces showing Garland and Minnelli, this deliberately artificial musical moment fits somehow – Allen is shown to be in control of the artifice, with his family dancing along in the lounge room at home.

Coda – Bringing Home the Tenterfield Saddler

In between the recreated pieces of Peter Allen's musical life in *The Boy From Oz*, there are touching imaginings of his writing processes for his two sentimental love letters, 'Tenterfield Saddler' and 'I Still Call Australia Home'. The first we see being written mostly in one sitting after Allen finds a newspaper obit written just after his grandfather passes – he scribbles on paper and tinkers at the small family upright piano until he gets the family story right. Marion asks him to "change the names, Pete", but he refuses, "No, Mum, it wouldn't be the same". Unlike the pieces of his musical life that were on screen at the time of his death (and have since been uploaded and reforwarded on YouTube and DVD), this is an intimate moment made more poignant by the dramatisation of the first part of the story earlier in the series. As with the other Jackson and Allen vocal performances, the vocal tone and timbre are similar, but not the same as the original, instead slightly syncopated. As the frame moves to a New York bar an image of Minnelli appears with the line "The grandson of George has been all around the world … he changed his last name and married a girl with an interesting face".

Throughout the miniseries the lyrics and melody of 'I Still Call Australia Home' are used to illuminate various moments of Allen's life. We hear him play something that sounds like a music box version of the tune just after he marries Liza, then again later to an approving ghostly Judy who gives him encouragement to continue to write. Finally, 'I Still Call Australia Home' is shown as Allen's last performance, singing in Sydney while sick but still in the infamous sequined Australian flag shirt that every Allen impersonator and actor since has also worn.

The musical moments in the miniseries are the ones that really strike. Peter Allen was *Not The Boy Next Door*; he was so much more beautiful than that.

CHAPTER 9

I Am Woman, Redux

Feminism on Television in 2015

MICHELLE ARROW

Just a few years ago, feminist writers and activists were despairing that most women were rejecting the label 'feminist'.[1] Yet today, it seems that feminism – and feminists – are everywhere. Some feminists – like Germaine Greer and Anne Summers – never went away. Others – like Julia Gillard – rediscovered their feminism in the face of unrelenting sexist vilification. Many more (including Annabel Crabb and Clementine Ford) have found receptive media spaces for their feminist analyses of contemporary Australia. Indeed, today feminism is largely understood not as a movement of activists whose activities are occasionally reported on *by* the media, but as a movement that happens in, and speaks *through*, the media.

Of course, this is not entirely unproblematic. The recent proliferation of 'women's' websites like *Daily Life*, *Mamamia* and *Women's Agenda*, which proclaim a broadly feminist orientation, are characterised by their emphasis on 'choice' feminism. As Clem Bastow noted, choice feminism is premised on "the idea that any choice a feminist makes is inherently a feminist act, any opinion they hold a feminist one".[2] The quest for web traffic to these sites tends to push their writing towards the confessional; the immediacy of the first person narrative forges a connection between writer and reader, but it doesn't necessarily become part of a push for feminist change.

---

1   'Girl Power', *The Australian*, August 30, 2008, www.theaustralian.com.au/arts/girl-power/story-e6frg8n6-1111117306604, accessed November 16, 2015.

2   Clem Bastow, 'I'm alright, Jill' *The Saturday Paper*, 4–10 April 2015, p.7.

While the feminist movement has long had an uneasy relationship with spokespeople and leaders, there is also a considerable history of feminist celebrities like Gloria Steinem, Anne Summers and Germaine Greer, women who proclaimed feminism in the media and became known as public faces of feminism.[3] Today, arguably our best-known feminists are making feminist television, even if they might not label it as such.

Yet the deployment of celebrity can be a double-edged sword. In July 2015 the *Sun-Herald* ran a story on the ABC's high-profile female journalists in their *Sunday Life* magazine. Entitled 'Screen Queens' and featuring a very heavily made-up Virginia Trioli, Leigh Sales and Emma Alberici on the cover, the story celebrated the ways that the "ABC's female journalists are changing the newsroom".[4] Arguing that women were driving the ABC's news agenda both on and off-screen, the story painted the ABC as an egalitarian haven for working mothers, with Sales recounting how the network's first female news director, Kate Torney, brought meals to her home when she was on maternity leave. Coming as it did on the back of the ABC's so-called 'hunger games' in late 2014, where dozens of journalists, many of them working mothers, had lost their jobs, this anecdote was spectacularly insensitive. A former ABC employee pointed out that such fantastically flexible working conditions were reserved only for the network's "stars"; none of these stars acknowledged their enormous privilege in the ensuing controversy.[5] This incident

---

3   Anthea Taylor, 'Germaine Greer's Adaptable Celebrity', *Feminist Media Studies* Vol. 14, No. 5, 2014, pp.759–774.

4   Erin O'Dwyer, 'How the ABC's female journalists are changing the newsroom', *Sunday Life*, 19 July 2015, www.dailylife.com.au/life-and-love/work-and-money/how-the-abcs-female-journalists-are-changing-the-newsroom-20150717-gif0dh.html.

5   Whitney Fitzsimmons 'The ABC a utopia for working mums? Sure, if you're one of the stars', *Crikey* 21 July 2015, www.crikey.com.au/2015/07/21/the-abc-a-utopia-for-working-mums-sure-if-youre-one-of-the-stars/.

revealed the limits of the personal narrative and celebrity as a way to raise feminist issues. It also encapsulated the insularity of much of what passes for feminist commentary in the media, with its focus on individual advancement at the expense of a more sustained, structural analysis.

Yet despite the dominance of an often-superficial media feminism, we might remember 2015 as a watershed year for feminism on television. Not because of our TV dramas: Australia still has a long way to go before we can hope to match the diversity and depth of American television's depiction of women (although many would argue it still has a long way to go as well).[6] But in 2015 the ABC broadcast programs that took gender inequality seriously and addressed it as an urgent social problem. In doing so, these programs have again affirmed the importance of public broadcasting as a national public space to discuss urgent social issues. These programs have also showcased television's unique power as a domestic medium to tell intimate stories. At their best, these programs reanimate an old second wave feminist idea – the personal is political.

The sharing of intimate stories has been a potent strategy of social movements since at least the 1970s. But how should women share such stories in a way that goes beyond the merely confessional? Of course, many feminists have been doing this online, but the fragmented audiences for social media means that these stories often resonate in an echo chamber of likes and shares, without having the national impact they require. Even as the audience for television splinters and timeshifts, television remains the most effective way to start a national conversation about important social and cultural issues. But can television produce change? In this essay I will focus on three programs from 2015 that broadcast feminist perspectives:

---

6   Zeba Blay, 'How Feminist TV became the new normal', 19 June 2015, www.huffingtonpost.com/2015/06/18/how-feminist-tv-became-the-new-normal_n_7567898.html.

Sarah Ferguson's two part series about domestic violence, *Hitting Home*, several episodes of the panel program *Q&A*, and the comedy series *Judith Lucy is all Woman*.

Judith Lucy is All Woman

Following the success of *Judith Lucy's Spiritual Journey* in 2011, in 2015 stand-up comedian Lucy utilised a similar formula of stunts, comedy, experiences and interviews to explore contemporary woman-hood in *Judith Lucy is All Woman*.[7] In six half-hour episodes, Lucy examined gender, work, relationships, sex, parenthood, mid-life and ageing, from the perspective of a white, forty-something, self-described feminist.

Throughout the series Lucy positioned herself as a feminist of the second wave variety, deeply sceptical of the raunch culture she sees as characteristic of contemporary young women. In an interview with musician Amanda Palmer, Lucy expresses surprise that singer Miley Cyrus would describe herself as a feminist, and in an interview to promote the series commented: "I guess I just didn't see Germaine Greer do a lot of twerking".

While Germaine may not have twerked, she did pose topless in *Oz* magazine in the late 1960s and her feminist politics of the 1970s were decidedly pro-sex.[8] Lucy's series was notable for the lack of space it gave to young women (though it did feature a couple of delightful group interviews with teenagers) and women of colour: indeed, the series ended with Lucy's advice to young women (rather than, say, giving young women space to offer advice to each other). The focus

---

7   *Judith Lucy is All Woman* (2015), a Bearded Lady/Pigeon Fancier Production, Presented by ABC and Film Victoria.

8   Lisa Featherstone and Haylee Ward, 'Pleasure, Pain, Power and Politics: Australian Feminist Responses to Pornography 1970–1989', in R. Reynolds, L. Featherstone and R. Jennings, eds, *Acts of Love and Lust: Sexuality in Australia from 1945–2010*, Cambridge Scholars Publishing, 2014, p.51.

on the experiences of older women, however, was welcome, as was her conversation with two trans men, Buck Angel and Jez Pez, who offered their reflections on life on both sides of the gender divide: women say sorry a lot more than men, they suggested, and men are happy to take up more space.

As ever in Lucy's comedy, she exposed herself to ridicule: across the series she appeared in her underwear, had a G-spot enhancement (interviewing the surgeon while he performed the procedure), and disguised herself as both a man and an elderly woman. Perhaps the series' most affecting moment was the touching rendition of Helen Reddy's feminist anthem 'I am Woman' by a group of Australian female singers: renewed in this way, the song proved that it still resonates.

While Lucy remained an appealing, deeply funny guide, the journey was presented entirely through her own perspectives and experiences. She was happy to own the label 'feminist' (as were many of the women she interviewed) but it was a feminism shorn of its radical potential, dispensing advice based on personal experience, rather than any broader social critique.

Hitting Home

'The personal is political' was one of the most radical ideologies of women's liberation. Coined by American feminist Carol Hanisch, the idea at its heart was simple: if you were a woman oppressed and disadvantaged, it wasn't just your problem to solve alone. Rather, the problems facing women – violence, harassment, self-image – were structural, products of a patriarchal society. Sharing such problems was the first step in trying to solve them.[9] From the late 1960s onwards, women met in groups to discuss their experiences of

---

9   Carol Hanisch, 'The Personal Is Political: The Women's Liberation Classic with a
    new explanatory introduction', 2006, http://carolhanisch.org/CHwritings/PIP.html.

education, sex, relationships, motherhood, and violence. Sometimes, these groups spilled over into larger gatherings that were part consciousness-raising, part demonstration. On International Women's Day 1973, Sydney Women's Liberation and the Women's Electoral Lobby organised the Sydney Women's Commission, where numerous women spoke to the crowd about their experiences of violence at the hands of their husbands and partners.[10] Anne Summers was one of the women there that day. She and some of her friends were so angered by what they heard that within months, they broke into two vacant houses owned by the Uniting Church in Glebe, squatted, and in 1974, established Elsie, Australia's first women's refuge. Elsie was soon overwhelmed with desperate women fleeing violent partners, and the refuge movement was born in Australia. Our response to domestic violence was, from the outset, one driven by feminists.

That the personal can still be political was clear when Rosie Batty became the 2015 Australian of the Year. Batty rose to national prominence in the most horrific way: her ex-partner, Greg Anderson, brutally murdered their eleven year old son Luke, in February 2013. By speaking publicly about her experience of family violence just days after Luke's death, Batty gave victims of such acts a rare public voice. She built momentum for a public conversation and has continued to do so since the award gave her a national profile. By speaking out, she refused the stigma and shame that typically attached itself to women in abusive relationships. Her public role was premised not on policy expertise, but her ability to speak from inside a violent relationship. "I am not a politician" she said. "What I have is personal experience".[11]

2015 saw unprecedented public attention paid to domestic and family violence in Australia. Rosie Batty's activism and the work

---

10 Nola Cooper, 'Sydney Women's Liberation Movement 1970-1975', Women's Health NSW, www.whnsw.asn.au/PDFs/The_Sydney_Womens_Liberation_Movement_1970-1975.pdf, accessed 25 November 2015.

11 Rosie Batty, 'Why passion must lead to change', *The Saturday Paper*, 7–13 February 2015.

of feminist activists over decades finally produced a conversation Australia had long avoided. The Counting Dead Women Project, undertaken by the feminist group Destroy the Joint, documented the deaths of more than 78 women due to domestic violence in 2015.[12] Journalist Jess Hill was nominated for a Human Rights Media Award for her clear-eyed, compelling reporting on domestic violence.[13] Former Governor-General Quentin Bryce convened a special taskforce into Domestic and Family Violence, and Victoria opened a Royal Commission into Family Violence on 22 February 2015.[14] Of course, this did not reverse the Federal and New South Wales governments' funding cuts to legal aid services, women's refuges and other services crucial to helping women escape violent relationships.[15] Neither has it stopped facile provocateurs like Mark Latham

---

12 The Counting Dead Women project totaled 78 for 2015 at the time of writing. See Moo Baulch, 'We've finally admitted we have a problem – now what?' *Daily Life*, 25 November 2015, www.dailylife.com.au/news-and-views/dl-opinion/moo-baulch-on-domestic-violence-weve-finally-admitted-we-have-a-problem--now-what-20151124-gl6pnq.html.

13 Jess Hill, 'Home Truths: the costs and causes of domestic violence', *The Monthly*, March 2015, www.themonthly.com.au/issue/2015/march/1425128400/jess-hill/home-truths.

14 *Not Now, Not Ever: Putting an end to Domestic and Family Violence in Queensland*, Report of the Special Taskforce on Domestic and Family Violence in Queensland, 2015, www.qld.gov.au/community/documents/getting-support-health-social-issue/dfv-report-vol-one.pdf; Royal Commission into Family Violence (Victoria), http://www.rcfv.com.au.

15 The Senate, Finance and Public Administration References Committee, *Domestic Violence in Australia Interim Report*, March 2015, www.aph.gov.au/senate_fpa; Jess Hill and Hagar Cohen, 'How funding changes in NSW locked women out of domestic violence refuges', *The Guardian*, 9 March 2015, www.theguardian.com/society/2015/mar/09/no-place-to-hide-how-women-are-being-locked-out-of-domestic-violence-refuges; Jenna Price, 'Australian of the Year Rosie Batty calls on PM Tony Abbott to reinstate community services', *Sydney Morning Herald*, February 1, 2015, www.smh.com.au/federal-politics/political-news/australian-of-the-year-rosie-batty-calls-on-pm-tony-abbott-to-reinstate-community-services-20150131-132o1n.html.

or Miranda Devine from suggesting that Rosie Batty was turning her story into "entertainment" or from arguing that the "the root causes of domestic violence are socio-economic", and "demonising men" is not the answer.[16] However, when Malcolm Turnbull announced a $100m funding injection for domestic violence services in September 2015 (a boost that nonetheless failed, according to the group Fair Agenda, to plug the system's significant funding gaps), he framed it in terms of gender inequality: "disrespecting women does not always result in violence against women. But all violence against women begins with disrespecting women".[17]

Hitting Home provided ample evidence of Turnbull's assertion. Produced by IN Films and broadcast by ABC1 on 24–25 November to strong ratings, *Hitting Home* was presented by journalist Sarah Ferguson.[18] *Four Corners* reporter Ferguson had gained heightened prominence when filling in as host of *7.30* while Leigh Sales was on maternity leave in 2013–14, crisply demolishing the carefully crafted media facades of various members of the Abbott government.[19] She applied this forensic precision to the mortifying soap opera that was the Rudd-Gillard-Rudd government in the series *The Killing*

---

16   Mark Latham, 'Mark Latham argues we are putting women in danger', *Australian Financial Review*, 27 June 2015, www.afr.com/opinion/columnists/mark-latham-argues-we-are-putting-women-in-danger-20150624-ghw6dx; Miranda Devine, 'Demonising Men Won't Stop Domestic Violence', *Daily Telegraph*, September 27, 2015, http://blogs.news.com.au/dailytelegraph/mirandadevine/index.php/dailytelegraph/comments/pm_disrespects_men_with_domestic_violence_stunt/.

17   Judith Ireland, 'Malcolm Turnbull's scathing attack on men who commit domestic violence', *Sydney Morning Herald*, September 24, 2015, www.smh.com.au/federal-politics/political-news/malcolm-turnbulls-scathing-attack-on-men-who-commit-domestic-violence-20150923-gjtpqt.html.

18   Nial Fulton and Ivan O'Mahoney (excecutive producers), *Hitting Home*, IN Films, ABC Television and Screen NSW, 2015.

19   Craig Matheson, 'Why Sarah Ferguson won't be easily forgotten as ABC's 7.30 presenter', *Sydney Morning Herald*, 30 May 2014, www.smh.com.au/entertainment/tv-and-radio/why-sarah-ferguson-wont-be-easily-forgotten-as-abcs-730-presenter-20140602-zrt8h.html.

Season, capturing the candid confessions of otherwise forgettable backbenchers as they boasted of their plotting prowess.

In *Hitting Home*, Ferguson cast her unflinching gaze on the victims and perpetrators of domestic violence, and on those who work in the systems that deal with this devastating problem. While women's stories of domestic violence are finding space in the public eye, we (understandably) hear little from the perpetrators of such crimes. *Hitting Home* not only revealed something of what it is like to live in an abusive relationship, it offered insights into male violence. Much of the series' power and authenticity stemmed from the access the producers gained to women's refuges, police officers, courts and prisons. As Ferguson noted in her introduction, while domestic violence has grown in public prominence more recently, "it's always been with us, hidden away like a dirty secret, and now we're finally paying attention". Ferguson went on:

> Like you I've watched those terrible stories but I've never really known what domestic violence really is. How does it start? How does it escalate from control to violence to death? Why do men do it – because it is largely men – and why do women stay with them?

These questions – especially "why doesn't she leave?" have long coloured public discussion of domestic violence, leaving a pall of shame and stigma on victims. It was *Hitting Home*'s significant achievement that it went some way to answering this question in a way that viewers could understand emotionally. To do this, the series foregrounded personal narratives, rather than expert talking heads. Statistics and information buttressed the arguments, but it was the intimate stories that were truly transformative, because they allow us to comprehend the emotional and social structures that perpetuate this kind of violence.

Ferguson noted that for those experiencing it, domestic violence is a deeply private trauma, and that "the private nature of it means people have been coy about it. It's part of a taboo … about what happens at home".[20] One of the aims of the series was to venture behind closed doors and speak to people living through these situations, rather than hearing from people reflecting on their experiences of some years earlier. Ferguson lived in a women's refuge for a time during production, which not only gave her a chance to meet and earn the trust of her vulnerable interviewees, but that she could take "people much closer to the events themselves, where the trauma of the event is present and alive".[21]

While several women's stories are told in episode one, two are told at length: those of Isabella and Wendy. Ferguson and her crew avoid the formal set-ups typical of current affairs reporting; instead, she talks to the women standing at kitchen benches, sitting on beds, whispering quietly over the bodies of the women's sleeping children. This lends the conversations a heartbreaking, quotidian intimacy. It also hands the women some agency in how they narrate their stories. Isabella recalls how she took responsibility for her partner's violence, recalling that she felt that she "had to do something better to make him happier", and that she was "embarrassed that I'd gotten into a relationship like this". It was only when her small son saw his father hit her that she felt she had to take action to protect her child. Ferguson talks to Isabella while security cameras are being installed at her house, there to record any attempts her husband might make to enter the family home, in breach of an Apprehended Violence Order (AVO: at the time the series was made, he was on bail awaiting trial for a violent assault on Isabella; we follow their case into the courts later in the episode). Perhaps the biggest revelation of these encounters is hearing the women explain why they persisted with

20 Paul Kalina, 'Sarah Ferguson tackles the domestic violence epidemic in Hitting Home', *Sydney Morning Herald*, 19 November 2015, www.smh.com.au/entertainment/tv-and-radio/sarah-ferguson-tackles-the-domestic-violence-epidemic-in-hitting-home-20151113-gkv2z9.html.

21 ibid.

relationships with violent men: Isabella says "I guess you're addicted to the hope that it's going to get better. And you don't want to be lonely … and it's hard if you have a child together". Later she realised if she didn't leave, she could be "one of those statistics". Watching Isabella testify in court against her unrepentant husband made for horrifying, gripping television.

Wendy's story of escape from a violent relationship into the safety of a women's refuge might have the biggest impact of all. Wendy marvels at how when she arrived at the refuge, everything was provided for her: toothpaste, shampoo, food and bed linen, the necessities of everyday life. Later she comments, "If I'd known how good it was I would have left the first time he yelled at me". However, as Silke Meyer pointed out, many women in desperate need are unable to access refuges: the program depicted 'ideal', rather than typical, frontline responses to domestic violence.[22] Wendy, like Isabella, remained in the relationship with her abusive partner because she wanted her children to have their father around, in spite of his violence. The series offered us chilling insights into the experience of family violence: we hear one of Wendy's triple 0 calls to police and it takes us into her terror: we hear the fury in her ex-partner's voice as he calls her a "fucking bitch". In these scenes, *Hitting Home* takes us to places many if not most will never see for themselves, building broader empathy and understanding. The series confronts the ways that violence impacts on children. Amidst snapshots of ordinary intimacies between mums and their children, we see Ferguson interview a shy, quiet boy about the "night mum's jaw was broken". He tells her that he wanted to do something but "I was only a ten year old kid". Afraid that his Dad "might come back and break my jaw", the boy tells Ferguson that "I want to go right up to his face and tell

---

22 Silke Meyer, 'ABC's Hitting home portrays ideal frontline responses to domestic violence', *The Conversation*, 24 November, 2015 https://theconversation.com/abcs-hitting-home-portrays-ideal-frontline-responses-to-domestic-violence-50121.

him "you're a very bad father"'. As Ferguson comments, women and children live in refuges because their homes are too dangerous, "and that's a situation we tolerate in Australia".

Episode two began with the problem facing victims of domestic violence: when do you decide to leave? How do you know when your life might be in danger? What makes a relationship turn violent? The series approaches these questions from a number of perspectives. First we meet the police working on the frontline of the domestic violence response. Police, we are told, are placing a greater emphasis on the risks posed to women once their partners turn violent. Second, we meet a group of perpetrators serving prison sentences, participating in a rehabilitation program. While the woman facilitating the group says that she sees "hope" when she looks around at the men in the group, it's hard to feel anything but deep unease when we see the ways these men refuse to take responsibility for the violence they perpetuate. What was most striking was the ways that they could not see (or acknowledge) the fear they provoked in their victims. Ferguson asks one perpetrator, Logan, "Are you frightening when you're angry?" "I don't think so", he replies.

Finally, the program seemed to negate any possible criticism that it was overly focused on violence in low socio-economic communities (the focus on Blacktown, for example) with the chilling story of Kate Malonyay, a successful young woman who lived in Mosman and who was brutally murdered by her ex-boyfriend, Elliott Coulson, in 2013. Kate's mother and close friends tell her story: she didn't think she was at risk, reassured her loved ones that Coulson would not hurt her. But he broke into her flat, killed her, and stayed there for two days before using her credit card to book a flight to Queensland. He committed suicide by jumping from the balcony of his hotel room when police arrived to arrest him. One of Kate's friends tells Ferguson that she didn't think that these kinds of horrors happened to "people like us". *Hitting Home* was such powerful television because it affirmed that domestic violence is overwhelmingly a gendered problem whose roots lay in the ways that men and women are conditioned to relate to each other. The final shot of the series was Ferguson holding a tiny baby boy in her arms, her description of this crisis as a "national emergency" ringing in her viewer's ears. The program captured the national conversation for a few short days and saw a spike in reporting of domestic violence: hopefully it will resonate in the national imagination for much longer.[23]

Performing the National Conversation: *Q&A*

In 2015, *Q&A* became a totem in the ongoing culture wars over public broadcasting in Australia. The ABC clearly prizes the program for the ways it performs participatory democracy: as Tony Jones says, it is "the show where you ask the questions", however carefully moderated and stage-managed this process might be.[24] The Abbott government thundered that "heads should roll" and ordered an inquiry into the program after former terrorism suspect Zaky Mallah was allowed to ask frontbencher Steve Ciobo about changes to citizenship laws (the infamous 'AbbottlovesAnal' twitter handle appearing on-screen just two months later didn't help matters either).[25] In a neoliberal political climate where the very existence of public broadcasting is

---

23 Bridget Brennan, 'Domestic violence support services record spike after ABC Documentary Hitting Home airs', December 3, 2015, http://www.abc.net. au/news/2015-12-03/surge-in-women-seeking-help-after-hitting-home-documentary-airs/6997764.

24 Terry Flew and Adam Swift, 'Engaging, Persuading and Entertaining Citizens: Mediatization and the Australian Political Public Sphere', *The International Journal of Press/Politics*, Vol. 20, No. 1, 2015, pp.119–120.

25 Latika Bourke and Matthew Knott, 'Q&A: Tony Abbott says "heads should roll" over Zaky Mallah episode, orders inquiry', *Sydney Morning Herald*, 25 June 2015, www.smh.com.au/federal-politics/political-news/qa-tony-abbott-says-heads-should-roll-over-zaky-mallah-episode-orders-inquiry-20150625-ghxeti. html#ixzz3t7vLkQhb; Neil McMahon, 'Q&A recap: Lewd Tony Abbott Twitter handle could put the show back in hot water', *Sydney Morning Herald*, 25 August

increasingly under question, *Q&A* demonstrates the ways that television can enact a virtual public sphere in which decision-makers can, theoretically, be held to account. The program's famed twitter feed often carries on a counter-conversation that disrupts or undercuts the conversation on the program, providing a background noise of humour, rage and cynicism.[26] More often than not, however, it is infuriating or deeply boring television, or both at the same time. The best political performers on *Q&A* (Malcolm Turnbull, Tanya Plibersek) are those who depart from their party-approved talking points to reveal something of themselves. Similarly, the best *Q&A* panels are usually those that move away from the typical focus on the week's news to stage a focused debate on a particular issue. The ABC broadcast its first all-female *Q&A* to commemorate International Women's Day in March, but the discussion was tired, or, in the case of Germaine Greer, even a little wacky (asking Julie Bishop if she would bare her nipples to free Andrew Chan and Muyran Sukumaran for example). As Gemma Munro wearily noted on *Women's Agenda*, "we just keep having the same conversations [about gender equality], over and over again. We seem to be banging our heads against the ultimate brick wall".[27] At its worst, *Q&A* simply rehashes debates already staged elsewhere. At its best it can marshal expertise, rather than just opinions, to move that debate forward.

In 2015 *Q&A* ran two episodes on domestic violence: one featuring Rosie Batty in February, and another immediately after *Hitting Home* in November. The first episode was made just weeks

---

2015, www.smh.com.au/entertainment/tv-and-radio/qa-recap-lewd-tony-abbott-twitter-handle-could-put-the-show-back-in-hot-water-20150825-gj6sdt.html.

26 Gay Hawkins, 'Enacting Public Value on the ABC's Q&A: From Normative to Performative Approaches', *Media International Australia*, No. 146, February 2013, p.90.

27 Gemma Munro, 'Why the first all-female Q&A missed the mark', *Women's Agenda*, 12 March 2015, www.womensagenda.com.au/talking-about/opinions/item/5442-why-the-first-all-female-q-a-missed-the-mark.

after Batty was named Australian of the year and she remained at the centre of the discussion throughout. The gendered (rather than socio-economic) framing of domestic violence has provoked controversy throughout the year and these tensions were apparent in both programs. Controversially, the first program included only two women (the other was Natasha Stott Despoja, Australia's Ambassador for Women and Girls), alongside two men who work on male behaviour change programs and the (male) Acting Victorian Police Commissioner. While Tony Jones defended the gender (im) balance by pointing out that men are a "key part of the problem", it didn't take long for the "not all men are violent" tweets to begin appearing on-screen as part of the broader *Q&A* conversation. While Stott-Despoja pointed out that domestic violence was still overwhelmingly perpetuated by men, the (false) statistic that one in three domestic violence victims are male was still circulating later in the year, when a young woman asked the panel to comment on it. By featuring experts with command of the data, the statistic was publicly debunked.[28] Similarly, Batty's willingness to be the 'face' of domestic violence, as an educated middle-class woman who "lived in a nice house", undermined the stereotype that violence is confined to the underclass in Australia. When her panel was asked "Why don't women leave?", she stopped the audience in its tracks with her direct but disarming response: "They don't want to leave – they just want … the violence to stop. Why would you want to leave your home, your family, the dreams that you've built?" It was perhaps evidence of some change that this question was not asked of the post-*Hitting Home Q&A*.

---

28 Jenny Noyes, 'One-in-three myth unanimously busted on "hitting Home" finale of Q&A', Daily Life, 26 November 2015, www.dailylife.com.au/dl-people/oneinthree-myth-unanimously-busted-on-hitting-home-finale-of-qa-20151125-gl8dzp.html.

Together, *Hitting Home* and *Q&A* attempted to provide audiences with both an emotional understanding of the horrors of intimate partner violence, and a broader sense of the policy and structural problems associated with responding to it. *Hitting Home* captured public attention for an entrenched social problem, one which feminists have campaigned about for decades. By investigating the experiences of those living within violent relationships, rather than highlighting service shortfalls, the series was able to suggest what drives this problem, and in doing so, it raised some profoundly disturbing questions about gender inequality in twenty-first century Australia. It was a powerful piece of feminist television.

Chapter 10

Mining for Drama

House of Hancock, *Gina Rinehart and the Law*

David Rolph

It began with Peta Sergeant as Rose Hancock (nee Lacson), bursting through white double doors into the entertaining area of Prix d'Amour, belting out Pat Benatar's 'Love is a Battlefield', to the evident distaste of her stepdaughter, Gina Rinehart, played by Mandy McElhinney. *House of Hancock*, a two-part miniseries about the lives of mining magnate, Lang Hancock, his daughter, Gina Rinehart, and his housekeeper-turned-wife, Rose Hancock, was one of the highest-rating dramas on Australian television in 2015. It was also one of the most controversial, with legal action almost delaying or stopping the second episode from being screened. The substantial audience for *House of Hancock* demonstrates again the appetite Australians have for dramas based on real people and events – a well-established genre in television here, dating back at least to landmark 1980s miniseries, such as *The Dismissal* and *Bodyline*. Despite the popularity of this genre, docudramas such as *House of Hancock* pose real legal risks to their makers and broadcasters, with defamation being the most prominent. Fictionalising aspects of a true story, whilst purporting to represent that true story, creates not only legal challenges but also challenges notions of journalistic and historical accuracy. Rather than focusing on the aesthetic merits of *House of Hancock*, this chapter will focus on the legal travails of the production. In particular, it will focus on the risks defamation action can pose to docudrama producers, particularly those trying to create entertaining and high-rating television from the lives of living (and litigious) people such as Gina Rinehart.

Production History

Aspects of Gina Rinehart's life have attracted media attention over several decades. Her family background and her wealth, as the only daughter of mining magnate Lang Hancock, meant that she was the subject of reporting from an early age. Through her own business activities, Rinehart became the richest person in Australia and, in 2012, with the price of iron ore high, she was named the richest woman in the world. In recent years, Rinehart has herself developed a public profile, intervening in public debates in support of conservative causes, such as opposing the mineral resources rent tax, the carbon pollution reduction scheme and its successor, the emissions trading scheme; advocating the development of northern Australia, particularly the creation of a special economic zone, and deregulation; and buying stakes in media companies Fairfax Media Ltd and Ten Network Holdings Ltd. However, it is her involvement in two long-running family legal battles which has made her of special interest to television screenwriters.

The level of interest in Gina Rinehart as a subject for a television programme is demonstrated by the fact that, in February 2013, not one but two separate projects based on her life were announced. The first was a six-hour miniseries, to be produced by Screentime Australia and based on the biography *Gina Rinehart: The Untold Story of the Richest Woman in the World*, by Fairfax journalist Adele Ferguson. The other was a four-hour miniseries, to be produced by Cordell Jigsaw Zapruder, for Channel Nine, with the working title *Mother Monster Magnate*. This production also had significant journalistic input behind it, with investigative journalist Steve Pennells being attached to the project. In 2012, Steve Pennells, then working for *The West Australian* newspaper, won the Gold Walkley Award for his coverage of Gina Rinehart's feud with her children over the multi-billion dollar family trust.[1] Initially, the Screentime production was not attached to a television network but eventually it became associated with Foxtel. Interestingly, its working title was *House of Hancock*.[2] Notwithstanding that it was announced first, the Screentime production appears to have gone into abeyance, with the Cordell Jigsaw Zapruder production proceeding and assuming the *House of Hancock* title.

A number of high-profile names were reported as being considered for the role of Gina Rinehart: Jacki Weaver, Gina Riley, Magda Szubanski.[3] Ultimately, however, Mandy McElhinney was cast.[4] McElhinney had an established relationship with Channel Nine, being the star of its 1960s hospital drama *Love Child*. Although initially famous for her recurring role as Rhonda in a series of advertisements for motor vehicle insurer AAMI, McElhinney had developed a substantial profile in Australian docudrama. She won the AACTA Award for Best Guest or Supporting Actress in a Television Drama for her portrayal of Kerry Packer's loyal, long-suffering secretary Rose, in Channel Nine's miniseries *Howzat! Kerry Packer's War*. Staying with the Packer publishing empire, she was nominated for the Logie Award for Most Outstanding Actress for her starring role as the colourful editor of *Woman's Day* magazine, Nene King, in

1 Holly Byrnes, 'Mother, monster, magnate Gina Rinehart's bitter battle with children will air in mini-series', *The Daily Telegraph*, 11 February 2013, p.5; Michael Idato, 'Race to televise Gina's story', *The Age*, 11 February 2013, p.3.

2 Michael Idato, 'Hancock-Rinehart drama to hit the small screen', *The Canberra Times*, 19 August 2013, p. 3; Holly Richards, 'Filming the Birth of a WA Business Dynasty', *The West Australian*, 20 August 2013, p. 2.

3 Michael Idato, 'Hancock-Rinehart drama to hit the small screen'; Holly Richards, 'Filming the Birth of a WA Business Dynasty', *The West Australian*, 20 August 2013, p.2.

4 Colin Vickery, 'Mandy turns mining magnate', *The Herald-Sun*, 14 August 2014, p.2.

the ABC's series *Paper Giants: Magazine Wars*. Subsequently, it was announced that Peta Sergeant would play Rose Hancock and Sam Neill would play Lang Hancock.[5]

At a relatively early stage of the production, it was decided that the miniseries should not deal with Gina Rinehart's current litigation with her children, which focuses on control over the Hope Margaret Hancock Trust. Instead, the focus of *House of Hancock* was to be on the relationship between Lang Hancock and Gina Rinehart from the 1960s onwards; Rinehart's two marriages; her emergence as a businesswoman in her own right; her hiring of Rose Lacson as a housekeeper for her father in 1983 after her mother's death; Lacson's marriage to Lang Hancock two years later; the acrimonious breakdown of the relationship between Lang Hancock and Gina Rinehart over his marriage to Rose; Gina Rinehart's contact with her Indigenous half-sister; and the fourteen-year legal feud between Gina Rinehart and Rose Hancock, after Lang Hancock's death, over his fortune.

Given the high profiles of the personalities and the events depicted, there was significant media anticipation about this series. In late August 2014 *The Daily Mail* published photographs taken by paparazzi of the actors arriving or leaving the set and of some of the stars in their characters' costumes. There was particular interest in McElhinney's physical transformation into the "noticeably fuller figured" Gina Rinehart. *The Daily Mail* suggested that producers were concerned to maintain secrecy about the production for fear of litigation from the Rinehart family.[6] However, the initial threat of litigation relating to *House of Hancock* was made on behalf of

---

5   Colin Vickery, 'Family millions and forbidden love', *The Sunday Times* (Perth), 17 August 2014, p.20.

6   Amy Croffey, 'From Rhonda to Rinehart! First look at a fuller figured Mandy McElhinney as Australia's richest woman Gina for telemovie The House of Hancock', *The Daily Mail* (Australia), 28 August 2014.

Rose Hancock. In January 2015 the trailer for *House of Hancock* was released.[7] Willie Porteous, the man Rose married following Lang Hancock's death, stated that he had sought legal advice after he had viewed the trailer, which he described as "highly defamatory and a work of fiction". He thought it "unfairly portrayed Rose as a seductress", particularly objecting to her being depicted doing a strip tease. Porteous indicated that he and Rose had offered to co-operate in the production to avoid any legal problems but Channel Nine refused. Rose and Willie Porteous did not act on their pre-publication threat but this was not the last one to be made in relation to *House of Hancock*. Channel Nine's concern about an injunction was such that it did not adopt its usual course of sending out preview DVDs for critics, instead inviting journalists to a screening at its premises.[8] As subsequent events would show, concern about litigation arising from *House of Hancock* was not misplaced.

The Broadcast of the First Episode and the Reaction

The first two-hour episode of *House of Hancock* was broadcast on Sunday 8 February 2015. It was a ratings success, being the second most watched program on the evening, beaten only by Channel Seven's reality television show, *My Kitchen Rules*. In the five metropolitan markets *House of Hancock* drew an overnight audience of 1.383 million viewers. Significantly, it rated higher than either of the two competing interviews with survivors of the Lindt Café siege, broadcast on Channel Nine's *60 Minutes* and Channel Seven's news

---

7   Marni Dixit, 'Channel Nine debuts new dramatic House of Hancock trailer featuring Mandy McElhinney as mining heiress Gina Rinehart and Sam Neill as her father Lang Hancock', *The Daily Mail* (Australia), 17 January 2015.

8   Siobhan Duck, 'Bid to stop Rose show', *The Herald-Sun*, 27 January 2015, p.12; Adele Ferguson, 'What's next for House of Hancock?', *The Australian Financial Review*, 9 February 2015, p.40.

special, *Inside the Siege: The Untold Story*.[9] Taking into account time-shifting over seven days, *House of Hancock* had a five-city audience of 1.563 million viewers. It was also the most time-shifted program of the evening.[10]

The critical reception to the first episode was mixed. Writing in *The Sydney Morning Herald*, Michael Lallo praised Mandy McElhinney's performance as Gina Rinehart, saying: "She has clinched Gina's boarding school accent; her repertoire of curt expressions; and her school-marmish, pull-up-your-socks attitude".[11] The dissonance between the advertisements, which seemed to promise a campy 1980s-style soap opera, and the program itself was also noted by critics. Influential television blogger David Knox wrote on his *TV Tonight* website that:

> [f]or a minute there I thought Nine had cancelled its reboot of *Return to Eden*, but when I spied the promos for *House of Hancock*, my faith was restored in over the top television. Big hair, big fashion, big histrionics and even a big bloody outback mine. It was the 1980s after all.

However, Knox went on to observe that *House of Hancock* was "actually more measured than the promos suggest" but ultimately concluded that: "Not taken too seriously, its 90 minutes is perfectly entertaining. If one looks for insight, however, it is harder to detect".[12]

The broadcast of the first episode prompted a strong response on behalf of Gina Rinehart. Even before it was broadcast, conservative

9   David Knox, 'Sunday 8 February 2015: Ratings', www.tvtonight.com.au/2015/02/sunday-8-february-2015.html.
10   David Knox, 'Timeshifted: Sunday 8 February 2015', www.tvtonight.com.au/2015/02/timeshifted-sunday-8-february-2015.html.
11   Michael Lallo, 'First look at House of Hancock, the epic story of Gina Rinehart, Lang Hancock and Rose Lacson', *The Sydney Morning Herald*, 2 February 2015.
12   David Knox, 'House of Hancock', www.tvtonight.com.au/2015/02/house-of-hancock.html.

columnist Miranda Devine slammed the series as a "trashy biopic". She said it "will dredge up painfully personal family feuds, to do with [Gina's] late father Lang Hancock's geriatric marriage to his Filipina maid".[13] Another controversial conservative columnist, Andrew Bolt, defended Rinehart on his blog:

> How many other women in this country have been subjected to the savage cruelty that Channel 9 has heaped on Gina Rinehart?
>
> Yes, I know she is very rich. Yes, I know she is conservative – a crime in polite circles.
>
> But she is also a human being. A woman.

Prefiguring the literal-mindedness of other complaints which would be made about *House of Hancock*, Bolt asked: "Was Channel Nine there? Does it know the truth of the savage claims it portrays as true?"[14]

Hancock Prospecting executive director, Tad Watroba, stated that he had written on three occasions to Channel Nine's chief executive officer, David Gyngell, about Rinehart's concerns over *House of Hancock*. Watroba was not satisfied that Channel Nine had undertaken proper fact-checking prior to the broadcast. He claimed that "many scenes broadcast were fictitious, unfounded or grossly distorted, and some simply never occurred". He characterised the program as "a tacky, disgraceful grab for ratings". A number of aspects of the first episode of *House of Hancock* were of particular concern to Rinehart. First, she rejected the portrayal of her being on her honeymoon and having to be recalled home while her mother

---

13 Miranda Devine, 'Trashy biopic slur to Gina', *Sunday Telegraph*, 8 February 2015, p.17.

14 Andrew Bolt, 'How can Channel 9 punch a woman like this?', 9 February 2015, http://blogs.news.com.au/heraldsun/andrewbolt/index.php/heraldsun/comments/how_can_channel_9_punch_a_woman_like_this/.

was dying. Secondly, she objected that she never supported or condoned deals with the Romanian dictator Nicolae Ceausescu, and did not "use a nuclear device for anti-environmental intent". Finally, she rejected the suggestion that her father had ever told her that no one could ever love her and that her husband had never loved her. In addition, to counter the allegation that Lang Hancock had made disparaging remarks about her weight, Rinehart released to the media a photograph of herself taken in the early 1990s, showing her then-slender figure.[15]

Rinehart's response provoked a defence. Interviewed on *A Current Affair*, one of the producers, Michael Cordell, described the source material as "an explosive *Dallas*-style drama". He claimed that "a lot of it we didn't have to make up, a lot of it is on the public record". Nevertheless, Cordell stated: "We're making a drama, we're not making a documentary".[16] This was a line echoed by Channel Nine's executive and legal teams in their correspondence with Rinehart's representatives, disclosed when Rinehart commenced legal proceedings.[17]

The Litigation Begins

Before the second episode of *House of Hancock* could be broadcast as scheduled on Sunday 15 February 2015, Rinehart commenced legal

---

15 Sharri Markson and Darren Davidson, 'The Diary', *The Australian*, 9 February 2015, p.24; Amanda Meade, 'Gina Rinehart aide slams Nine's "tacky" dramatisation of Hancock dynasty', *The Guardian* (Australia), 10 February 2015; Richard Noone, 'House of Hogwash', *The Daily Telegraph*, 10 February 2015, p.11.

16 Danielle Gusmaroli, "'It's an explosive Dallas-type drama grounded in truth": House of Hancock director Michael Cordell hits back at Gina Rinehart's claims hit TV show is "tacky"', *The Daily Mail* (Australia), 11 February 2015; Amanda Meade, 'Gina Rinehart wins permission to watch The House of Hancock early', *The Guardian* (Australia), 13 February 2015.

17 *Rinehart v Nine Entertainment Co Holdings Ltd* [2015] NSWSC 239, [12]-[13] (Garling J).

proceedings in the Supreme Court of New South Wales against Channel Nine. She sought an order for preliminary discovery; specifically access to a preview copy of the second episode, in order to determine whether she should seek an injunction to restrain the broadcast. The matter was given an urgent hearing before Garling J only two days before the second episode of the miniseries was to be aired. The principal causes of action Rinehart relied upon were defamation and injurious falsehood. A cause of action for misleading or deceptive conduct was faintly raised in argument. When counsel for Rinehart suggested in court that a professional paid actor could be engaged in misleading or deceptive conduct, Garling J described the submission as "a novel proposal", one which "would shut down all of Shakespeare's plays".[18] Dealing with the application for preliminary discovery based principally on defamation, Garling J found that there was a real issue as to whether the second episode contained inaccurate materials, given the evidence in relation to the miniseries as a whole, and therefore there was a real issue as to whether the second episode conveyed defamatory imputations about Rinehart.[19] Ordinarily, it is extremely difficult to get an injunction to stop a defamatory publication.[20] Courts in Australia, as in other common law countries, have long been averse to prior restraint.[21] People usually can exercise freedom of speech though, in so doing, must accept the legal consequences. His Honour took into account the principle of free speech but noted that it was not absolute.[22] Balancing all these

---

18   Louise Hall, Jenna Clarke and Michael Lallo, 'Rinehart threatens to block biopic', *The Sydney Morning Herald*, 14 February 2015, p.3; Amanda Meade, 'Gina Rinehart wins permission to watch The House of Hancock early'.

19   *Rinehart v Nine Entertainment Co Holdings Ltd* [2015] NSWSC 239, [56] (Garling J). See also ibid, [26]-[28].

20   David Rolph, 'Showing Restraint: Interlocutory injunctions in defamation cases' (2009) 14 *Media and Arts Law Review* 255 at 275.

21   *Australian Broadcasting Corporation v O'Neill* (2006) 227 CLR 57 at 86-87 per Gummow and Hayne JJ; [2006] HCA 46.

22   Ibid, [57].

discretionary considerations, Garling J held that Rinehart should be granted access to a preview copy of the second episode of *House of Hancock*.[23] Given the short period of time between the hearing and the proposed broadcast, his Honour ordered Rinehart to notify the Court and Channel Nine by the evening of its intention to seek a pre-publication injunction.[24]

Having viewed the second episode of *House of Hancock*, Rinehart decided to apply for an injunction. The hearing of the application occurred at midday on Saturday 14 February 2015, the day before the scheduled broadcast. Weekend sittings of the Supreme Court are extremely rare. The parties appeared at the hearing but had already been involved in talks with a view to reaching a settlement. After two hours and two adjournments by Garling J to allow the talks to continue, the parties reached a confidential settlement. The broad outline of the settlement was revealed but not the details. Under the terms of settlement, Channel Nine agreed to excise certain parts of the second episode of *House of Hancock* and to place a disclaimer at the beginning of the broadcast, emphasising that what followed was a drama, not a documentary, and that certain events had been fictionalised. Rinehart reserved her right to pursue a claim for damages for defamation and injurious falsehood.[25]

Channel Nine made the agreed changes and added the disclaimer so that the broadcast of the second episode was able to go ahead as scheduled. One of the most fascinating aspects of the second episode of *House of Hancock* was not dramatised but real. Towards the end of

---

23   Ibid, [62].

24   Ibid, [66].

25   Brenden Hills, 'Gina made Nine fix Hancock TV biopic', *The Sunday Telegraph*, 15 February 2015, p.19; Linda Morris, 'Rinehart reaches settlement with Nine over TV mini-series', *The Canberra Times*, 15 February 2015, p.3; Jamelle Wells and Claire Aird, 'Gina Rinehart and Channel Nine reached confidential agreement on House of Hancock TV series', *Australian Broadcasting Corporation News* (online), 14 February 2015.

the episode, footage was included of Jana Wendt's 1985 *60 Minutes* interview with Lang and Rose Hancock. This gave viewers an insight into the real Lang and Rose Hancock and a comparator by which to assess at least some of the performances in *House of Hancock*. The footage reinforced how truly bizarre the source material actually was.

Unsurprisingly, Rinehart's legal proceedings against Channel Nine generated considerable publicity. This ensured that the second episode of *House of Hancock* was as successful as the first in terms of ratings. It attracted 1.38 million viewers across the five major cities based on overnight figures. On this measure, it was the second highest rating program on that night, again beaten only by *My Kitchen Rules*.[26] It attracted 1.64 million viewers when the seven-day time-shifted figures were factored in, making it the most watched program on the night.[27]

Because the terms of the settlement were confidential, it is not definitely known what all the changes to the second episode were. As Linda Morris observed in *The Canberra Times*: "At what cost to dramatic integrity only the producers and possibly a handful of critics will know". *The Courier-Mail* reported that Rinehart objected to the closing scene in which "a present-day Rinehart (played by Mandy McElhinney) lumbers slowly across the red dirt of the Pilbara. Behind her, explosions rock the landscape". It also reported that Rinehart objected to the inclusion of reference to a sexual harassment case brought against her by a former security guard, which was settled out of court, and a scene in which she berates her daughter for reading a magazine with Rinehart on the cover.[28] *The Australian* reported that Rinehart also objected to the suggestion that she confronted Rose Hancock over her relationship with Lang, given that they rarely

---

26 David Knox, 'Sunday 15 February 2015: Ratings', www.tvtonight.com. au/2015/02/sunday-15-february-2015.html.

27 David Knox, 'Timeshifted: Sunday 15 February 2015', www.tvtonight.com. au/2015/02/timeshifted-sunday-15-february-2015.html.

28 'Not scene or heard', *The Courier-Mail*, 16 February 2015, p.15.

spoke; the suggestion that Lang Hancock intended Gina's son, John Hancock, to take over the family's mining business; and the depiction of her talking to her deceased father, which she claimed made her appear to be of questionable sanity. Rinehart was not the only one who was aggrieved by their depiction in the second episode of *House of Hancock*. John Hancock told *The Australian* that he was portrayed as Lurch, the butler from *The Addams Family*, and denied that he was sent to the Philippines by his mother, having never visited that country.[29] Others, like Rose Porteous, may also have had reason to be upset by the way in which they were presented. However, it was only Rinehart who took legal action.

From what can be gleaned from the media reporting, Rinehart's objections were to the way in which people were depicted, not that the program was defamatory *per se*. Many stressed that aspects of the program were fictitious and therefore untrue; that aspects of the program did not happen in the way they were depicted; conversations were not had as shown, words were not said or exchanged, people did not act in the way they were portrayed. These objections overlooked or refused to accept the nature of the program: that *House of Hancock* was a docudrama, not a documentary, and that, as a consequence, aspects of the program were fictionalised for dramatic effect. This highlights then a fundamental tension in docudrama as a genre. On the one hand, docudrama necessarily takes licence with the given facts – it seeks to dramatise events. On the other hand, the authenticity of docudrama requires that it is still sufficiently grounded in fact.

Further Litigation

The legal action did not end with the broadcast of the second episode. Rinehart commenced proceedings against Channel Nine in the

---

29 Leo Shanahan, 'Gina's cuts "not for accuracy", *The Australian*, 17 February 2015, p.3.

Supreme Court of New South Wales for defamation and injurious falsehood. In addition to damages, Rinehart was concerned to prevent the material edited out of the broadcast being included on the DVD release.[30] In mid-June 2015, however, Rinehart signalled her intention to discontinue her proceedings against Channel Nine. Instead, she is now suing the production company, Cordell Jigsaw Zapruder.[31] She is reportedly suing for misleading or deceptive conduct, injurious falsehood and invasion of privacy.[32] Pursuing claims for misleading or deceptive conduct and injurious falsehood, but not defamation, against a media outlet, is unusual because defamation is much easier for a plaintiff to establish than the other causes of action. All a plaintiff has to establish in order to sue for defamation is that the defendant published material which disparaged his or her reputation and that the plaintiff was indirectly identified by the material. Damage to the plaintiff's reputation is then presumed and the defendant has to establish a defence. In order to obtain a remedy for injurious falsehood and misleading or deceptive conduct, a plaintiff would need to prove actual damage.

The other cause of action – invasion of privacy – is particularly interesting. Although there may be a widespread perception that invading another person's privacy is against the law, there is no direct, general protection of privacy under Australian law. Over the last thirty years, other common law legal systems, such as the United Kingdom and New Zealand, have begun to develop legal means

---

30 Michael Bodey, 'Rinehart to sue Nine over series', *The Australian*, 2 March 2015, p.23; Louise Hall, 'Rinehart to sue Nine for defamation over TV series', *The Sydney Morning Herald*, 2 March 2015, p.2; Amanda Meade, 'Gina Rinehart moves to stop release of uncut House of Hancock DVD', *The Guardian* (Australia), 2 March 2015.

31 Louise Hall, 'Rinehart to sue House of Hancock producers', *The Sydney Morning Herald*, 20 June 2015, p.15; Marianna Papadakis, 'Rinehart mounts claim against Nine', *The Australian Financial Review*, 18 July 2015, p.6.

32 Marianna Papadakis, 'Rinehart mounts claim against Nine', *The Australian Financial Review*, 18 July 2015, p.6.

of protecting privacy. In 2001, in *Australian Broadcasting Corporation v Lenah Game Meats Pty Ltd*, the High Court of Australia tantalisingly hinted it was receptive to arguments seeking to develop Australian law on privacy protection.[33] It is fifteen years since that decision, yet there have been only two judgements by inferior courts recognising a cause of action for invasion of privacy under Australian law.[34] Both cases were brought by private individuals. A significant reason that English privacy law has developed so rapidly over the same period is that celebrities have been willing to litigate in that country. Naomi Campbell, Michael Douglas and Catherine Zeta-Jones, Prince Charles, Max Mosley, J.K. Rowling, Boris Johnson and sundry English Premier League footballers, to name but a few, have all sued for misuse of private information, the form of direct privacy protection being developed by English law.[35] No high-profile Australian has thus far sued to final judgement for invasion of privacy in Australian courts. Rinehart's litigation against Cordell Jigsaw Zapruder may prove to be the test case for which Australian lawyers have been waiting. The outcome of the proceedings will not be known until at least 2016. Rinehart has to file her affidavit evidence by early 2016.[36] The legal consequences of *House of Hancock* may yet extend by the year of its broadcast.

---

33 (2001) 208 CLR 199 at 225-26 per Gleeson CJ, at 250 per Gummow and Hayne JJ; [2001] HCA 63.

34 *Grosse v Purvis* (2003) Aust Torts Reports 81-706; [2003] QDC 151; *Doe v Australian Broadcasting Corporation* [2007] VCC 281.

35 See, for example, *Campbell v MGN Ltd* [2004] 2 AC 457; *Douglas v Hello! Ltd* [2006] QB 125; *HRH Prince of Wales v Associated Newspapers Ltd* [2008] Ch 57; *Mosley v News Group Newspapers Ltd* [2008] EWHC 1777 (QB); *Murray v Express Newspapers plc* [2009] Ch 481; *AAA v Associated Newspapers Ltd* [2013] EWCA Civ 554. The cases involving footballers are too numerous to mention.

36 Marianna Papadakis, 'Setback for Rinehart's case against Channel Nine', *The Australian Financial Review*, 19 September 2015, p.10.

Litigation is not the only way to seek to manage reputation. Indeed, it is a peculiarly ineffective means of doing this.[37] Although notoriously media-shy, Gina Rinehart agreed to appear on a two-part episode of the ABC's *Australian Story* program in July 2015. The episodes, collectively called 'Iron, Iron, Iron: The Hancock Dynasty', allowed Rinehart to tell her story from her perspective. Broadcast on 6 and 13 July, they were unlikely to have occurred without the impetus of *House of Hancock*.[38]

Australian Docudramas: Legal, Historical and Journalistic Issues

Television drama is expensive to produce. Its expense makes it an unappealing investment for commercial Australian television networks, required by the Australian Content Standard to screen minimum levels of new Australian drama each year. According to Screen Australia's most recent report on drama, in 2014–15, there were forty-seven Australian dramas on television, spanning 517 hours and reflecting an investment of $299 million. This represented a decrease from 2013–14, when television networks broadcast fifty-one Australian dramas across 603 hours, reflecting an investment of $343 million.[39] Given the expense and risk involved in Australian television drama it is understandable that Australian television networks and producers are drawn to docudrama. The genre has the advantage that the people and events are usually known to at least a substantial proportion of the audience.

---

37 David Rolph, *Reputation, Celebrity and Defamation Law*, Ashgate, Aldershot, 2008, p.184.

38 See www.abc.net.au/austory/content/2015/s4265362.htm; www.abc.net.au/austory/content/2015/s4269824.htm.

39 Screen Australia, *Drama Report: Production of feature films and TV drama in Australia 2014/15*, p.10, www.screenaustralia.gov.au/getmedia/751abb13-3e15-4772-863f-5bf27f4760a3/dramareport.pdf.

House of Hancock was not the only high-rating Australian docu-drama screened in 2015. In May of that year Channel Seven broadcast *Catching Milat*, about the notorious 'Backpacker Murderer', Ivan Milat. In September the same network broadcast *Peter Allen: Not the Boy Next Door*, and in November Channel Ten broadcast *Mary: The Making of a Princess*, a telemovie about how Mary Donaldson from Tasmania met and married Crown Prince Frederik of Denmark. Over the past eight years, commercial networks and public broad-casters alike, free-to-air and pay television, have released a substantial number of docudramas, including: *Hawke* (2010); *Killing Time* (2011); *Paper Giants: The Birth of Cleo* (2011); *Beaconsfield* (2012); *Howzat! Kerry Packer's War* (2012); *Underground: The Julian Assange Story* (2012); *Paper Giants: Magazine Wars* (2013); *Carlotta* (2014); *INXS: Never Tear Us Apart* (2014); *Schapelle* (2014); and seven years of *Underbelly*, from 2008 onwards. The programs' and producers' interest in docudramas shows no sign of abating, with Channel Seven already promoting its next fact-based miniseries, based on the life and times of *Countdown* presenter and Australian music legend, Ian 'Molly' Meldrum. Biopics based on Paul Hogan, Olivia Newton-John and Peter Brock are also in development for 2016. It seems that no celebrity life story will not be considered for screening to audiences.

Like *House of Hancock*, many of these docudramas have occasioned legal controversy. The first series of *Underbelly*, depicting the Mel-bourne gangland wars, in which thirty-six underworld figures were killed between 1998 and 2010, was suppressed by court order in Victoria so as not to prejudice Evangelos Goussis's trial for the mur-der of Lewis Moran.[40] Even after the conviction of Goussis for this

---

40 See *X v General Television Corporation Pty Ltd* (2008) 187 A Crim R 33 at 541 per Vickery J; *General Television Corporation v Director of Public Prosecutions* (2008) 19 VR 68 at 88 per curiam. See also David Rolph and Jacqueline Mowbray, '"It's A Jungle Out There": The Legal Implications of *Underbelly*' (2009) 18(1) *Communications Law Bulletin* 10 at 13.

crime, the arrest and extradition of Tony Mokbel back to Victoria meant that the uncut version of *Underbelly* could only be broadcast and released on DVD in Victoria three years after it had been aired throughout the rest of Australia. *Killing Time* also encountered legal difficulties due to its potential prejudice of a criminal trial. The series dealt with the spectacular fall from grace of high-profile criminal defence lawyer Andrew Fraser, played by David Wenham. The initial airing on pay television channel TV1, was delayed due to a concern that it would prejudice the trial of Peter Dupas for the 1997 murder of Mersina Halvagis.[41] The subsequent rebroadcast of *Killing Time* on free-to-air network Channel Seven was the subject of an application for an injunction. Dupas unsuccessfully tried to have the rebroadcast stopped on the basis that he had an appeal against his conviction and sentence pending and, if the appeal were allowed, there would be a retrial which might be prejudiced.[42]

The legal risk most frequently posed by docudramas, though, is defamation. The second entry in the *Underbelly* franchise, *The Golden Mile*, raised a similar issue to that in the *House of Hancock* litigation. Former Kings Cross police officer, Wendy Hatfield, suspected that a character based on her in the series defamed her. She sought access to the episodes prior to screening. (The character, 'Wendy Jones', was shown having a sexual relationship with colourful Kings Cross identity John Ibrahim, whilst she was a serving political officer.) She was refused access to the tapes and had to wait until the episodes were broadcast.[43] Hatfield then sued for defamation. The claim against Channel Nine was eventually settled.[44] She also sued separately the publisher of the tie-in book, for defamation, and reportedly settled

41 Karl Quinn, 'True crime drama pulled from schedule over legal fears', *The Sydney Morning Herald*, 11 August 2010.

42 *Dupas v Channel Seven Melbourne Pty Ltd* [2012] VSC 486 at 24 per Kyrou J.

43 *Hatfield v TCN Channel Nine Pty Ltd* (2010) 77 NSWLR 506 at 531 per McColl JA.

44 Lisa Davies, 'Former police officer Wendy Hatfield claims court victory over Underbelly', *The Daily Telegraph* (Sydney), 15 November 2011.

those proceedings on equally favourable terms.[45] *Paper Giants: The Birth of Cleo* also encountered defamation problems, again due to thinly veiled fictionalisation of a character. Alasdair Macdonald, Ita Buttrose's ex-husband, sued the ABC for defamation over the way in which he was portrayed in the series and, specifically, their marriage breakdown. In the series, his character was simply referred to as 'Mac', but this did not stop him from being identifiable. The ABC settled the proceedings on confidential terms, also apologising unreservedly to Macdonald in open court.[46]

House of Hancock spurred a debate about the ethics of docudrama. The former host of *Media Watch*, Jonathan Holmes, writing in *The Age*, asked "what, exactly, are these series? Are they fact or fiction?" He complained that there is no way for the viewer to distinguish between the two. Consequently, Holmes had no sympathy for the legal travails the network and the producers found themselves in. In Holmes' view, *House of Hancock* "broke one of the fundamental ethical rules of real-life drama: it was made without the consent of its principal characters". He argued that, although the public may be interested in the lives of Lang Hancock, Gina Rinehart and Rose Porteous, there was no legitimate public interest in their story. In his view, people portrayed thus had only one option, which was to sue for defamation, and they were entitled to do so.[47] Television critic for *The Age*, Debi Enker, writing in 'The Green Guide', responded that Holmes' view was "an ill-considered position, one that would never be applied to newsgathering, current affairs coverage, or unauthorised biographies". However, none of the genres Enker cites claims to have a dramatised or fictionalised element to them. More convincingly,

45   Lisa Davies, 'Ex-cop Wendy Hatfield wins Underbelly cash payout', *The Daily Telegraph* (Sydney), 22 December 2010.

46   Louise Hall, 'ABC apology to Buttrose's ex-husband read in court', *The Sydney Morning Herald*, 30 April 2012.

47   Jonathan Holmes, 'Real-life TV stories need to get the facts right', *The Age*, 25 February 2015, p.45.

Enker pointed to the long cinematic tradition of the biopic, of which *The Queen*, *The Social Network*, *Chopper* and *The Iron Lady* were the most recent examples.[48]

Television biopics are likely to be a mainstay of programming well into the future. Australian audiences have demonstrated their appetite for seeing such stories. Inevitably, though, the legal issues and ethical debates which accompany real-life dramas are also bound to continue.

---

48 Debi Enker, 'Real-life TV a risky business', *The Age*, 'Green Guide', 19 March 2015, p.6.

Dramatising Australia's Colonisation

White Men's Stories in Banished *(BBC/Foxtel) and* The Secret River *(ABC TV)*

SARAH PINTO

Since the 1990s Gallipoli has come to signify the nation's involvement in the First World War and the birth of its ostensibly true national character. Perhaps unsurprisingly, then, Australian historical television in 2015, the centenary year of the much-mythologised Gallipoli landing, has been preoccupied with stories of the war. Amid the endless First World War depictions and dissections, however, were two pieces of historical television that offered viewers an alternative Australian beginning. The historical dramas *Banished* (BBC/Foxtel) and *The Secret River* (ABC TV) portrayed the colonisation of New South Wales, a relatively unusual focus for Australian historical television in the twenty-first century.[1]

The Secret River was a highly-anticipated production based on Kate Grenville's 2005 historical novel.[2] Grenville's novel was a phenomenon: a popular, controversial, and prize-winning best-seller that spawned two further novels and a theatrical production before its miniseries.[3] The story is loosely based on the life of Grenville's

---

1 For an overview see Michelle Arrow, 'Broadcasting the Past: Australian Television Histories', *History Australia* Vol. 8, No. 1, 2011, pp.223–46.

2 Kate Grenville, *The Secret River*, Text, Melbourne, 2005.

3 Kate Grenville, *The Lieutenant*, Text, Melbourne, 2008; Kate Grenville, *Sarah Thornhill*, Text, Melbourne, 2011; Andrew Bovell, *The Secret River, by Kate Grenville: An Adaptation for the Stage*, Currency Press, Sydney, 2013. There has been significant and varied interest in Grenville's *Secret River* from both historians and literary studies scholars. For discussions of this interest see Martin Staniforth,

ancestor Solomon Wiseman, and follows encounters between settlers and Indigenous peoples along the Hawkesbury River in 1810. *Banished*, in contrast, arrived on Australian screens unexpectedly. A BBC production written by the well-known screenwriter Jimmy McGovern, *Banished* was first screened in the UK to mixed reviews.[4] The seven-part series depicted two weeks at Sydney Cove in 1788, focusing on the daily struggles of the convict population. It had a wider purchase in Australia than its screening on the cable network Foxtel might suggest, mostly because of its puzzling exclusion of Indigenous characters. A second season – this time with Indigenous storylines – was intended for 2016, but was then abandoned.[5]

Although telling similar stories of British colonisation in Australia, the two productions are very different. In *The Secret River* the central drama of Australia's origins is the clash between European and Indigenous peoples over land. The emancipated convict William Thornhill (Oliver Jackson-Cohen) claims land along the banks of the Hawkesbury, settling there with his wife Sal (Sarah Snook) and their children. Although Sal longs for a return to London, Will is intoxicated by the land along the river, which he names Thornhill's Point. For Will the land is an opportunity for wealth, stability, and freedom: "That's my pardon", he says to Sal, "and there ain't no other damn freedom like it". But his desire for it cannot erase Indigenous ownership, and the Thornhills' presence along the Hawkesbury does

---

'Depicting the Colonial Home: Representations of the Domestic in Kate Grenville's *The Secret River* and *Sarah Thornhill*, *Journal of the Association for the Study of Australian Literature* Vol. 13, No. 2, 2013, p.1; and Robert Clarke and Marguerite Nolan, 'Book Clubs and Reconciliation: A Pilot Study on Book Clubs Reading the "Fictions of Reconciliation"', *Australian Humanities Review* 56, 2014, pp.122–23.

4   John Plunkett, 'Banished Leads BBC2 to Ratings Victory with More Than 3m Viewers', *The Guardian*, 6 March 2015, accessed 2 November 2015, www.theguardian.com/media/2015/mar/06/banished-bbc2-ratings-victory-russell-tovey.

5   'The Official Line on Banished', BBC One Points of View, accessed 2 November 2015, www.bbc.co.uk/programmes/articles/3rmPkvqynL8F9hwzQPRymB4/the-official-line-on-banished.

not easily displace the local Dharug peoples. A sense of inevitability fuels the subsequent violent conflict between Will and the other Hawkesbury settlers and the local peoples. A bloody and visceral massacre of Indigenous men, women and children is *The Secret River*'s climactic scene, and its aftermath is full of metaphorical significance for the contemporary Australian nation.

As my re-telling of the miniseries perhaps suggests, *The Secret River* is a beautiful piece of historical television. Its self-conscious sense of importance is enticing, although for viewers with a substantial knowledge of Australia's past there isn't much new here. The high production values and quality cast reference the landmark period dramas of the Revival of the Australian film industry in the 1970s and 1980s.[6] And there are moments that evoke other images of Australian identity, suggesting a production very deliberately engaged in a national project. These gestures explain why scholars often connect television with national identity; *The Secret River* seems to take this connection very seriously.[7]

The Secret River's nation-making project was reinforced by discussions of the miniseries in the Australian media, where it was lauded as a ground-breaking account of Australia's origins, a "sumptuous", "accurate", "nuanced", "remarkable", and "courageous" rendering of an "uncomfortable" history.[8] Graeme Blundell echoed many of the

---

6   On the Revival see Tom O'Regan, *Australian National Cinema*, Routledge, London, 1996.

7   For a discussion of television and the nation see Jerome de Groot, *Remaking History: The Past in Contemporary Historical Fictions*, Routledge, London, 2016, p.49.

8   "sumptuous": Fiona Purdon, 'River of Dreams', *The Courier-Mail*, 13 June 2015, p.23; "accurate": attributed to Aunty Edna Watson by Lauren Tesolin, 'Unsettling Truth of Our Grim Past', *Penrith Press*, 3 July 2015, p.12; "nuanced": Andrew Fenton, 'Race Against Time', *Sunday Herald Sun*, 14 June 2015, p.1; "remarkable": Michael Cathcart speaking on Books and Arts, Radio National, 19 June 2015, accessed 3 November 2015, www.abc.net.au/radionational/programs/booksandarts/the-secret-river/6556896; "courageous": Paul Daley, '*The Secret River* Review: Have We Really Moved On?', *The Guardian*, 15 June 2015, accessed

reviews when he called the production "seriously good television" that did "full justice" to Grenville's novel.[9] Indeed, Paul Daley placed the miniseries at the centre of an anticipated national "reckoning" with this past.[10] This kind of congratulatory commentary was widespread but not universal: Scott Rankin, for example, described *The Secret River* – as miniseries, play, and novel – as a "dangerous" text that turns non-Indigenous histories of encounter into "*the* history" of encounter, effectively and problematically sidelining Indigenous perspectives.[11] But most discussion emphasised *The Secret River*'s importance, and strong audience numbers suggested viewers agreed.[12]

Banished received a very different treatment. The series was derided in reviews and commentary in the UK and Australia. It was called a "grubby little drama" that pours on melodrama "more thickly than the tv crew's sun cream".[13] Its storylines were likened to the worst of reality television, akin to 'I'm a Convict Get Me Out of Here'.[14] And Ruth Ritchie suggested a more appropriate title for the series might have been 'True Love Amidst a Good Flogging'.[15] In Australia the strongest criticisms were over the lack of Indigenous characters, a

2 November 2015, www.theguardian.com/tv-and-radio/2015/jun/15/the-secret-river-review-have-we-really-moved-on; "uncomfortable": Graeme Blundell, 'Fish Out of Water', *The Australian*, 13 June 2015, p.23.

9   Blundell, 'Fish Out of Water'.

10 Daley, 'The Secret River Review'.

11 Scott Rankin speaking on Books and Arts.

12 Michael Bodey, 'ABC Miniseries Delivers Best Sunday Audience for Year', *The Australian*, 15 June 2015, accessed 2 November 2015, www.theaustralian.com.au/business/media/abc-miniseries-delivers-best-sunday-audience-for-year/story-e6frg996-1227398578858.

13 "grubby little drama": 'What to Watch', *The Daily Telegraph*, 28 February 2015, p.48; "more thickly than the tv crew's sun cream": Ceri Radford, 'This Penal Colony Drama Was Grim and Heavy-Handed', *The Daily Telegraph*, 6 March 2015, p.32.

14 Sam Wollaston, 'Banished Review: 18th Century Australia or I'm a Convict Get Me Out of Here?', *The Guardian*, 6 March 2015, p.29.

15 Ruth Ritchie, 'Of Frauds and Floggings', *Sydney Morning Herald*, 4 July 2015, p.38.

criticism so widespread that it prompted McGovern to pen a defence in the *Sydney Morning Herald*.[16] Troy Bramston's condemnation of the "glaring omission" of Indigenous Australians from the story as "simply unbelievable" encapsulated much of the extensive public commentary.[17]

The absence of Indigenous characters makes *Banished* very odd viewing, made even more odd by the sometime focus on Governor Arthur Phillip (David Wenham), whose relationships with the local Eora peoples are well-known; by a storyline that includes a main character, James Freeman (Russell Tovey), absconding from the settlement and into the bush; and by acknowledgements of thanks to the 'Guringai People' and the 'Dharawal Nation' in the series credits. McGovern offered several explanations, including the added time and cost of including Indigenous stories, the storyline's short two-week timeframe, and the series' British origins.[18] But none of these explanations seemed even close to sufficient in 2015-Australia, and the notion that the story of British settler colonialism for British audiences doesn't require Indigenous peoples was frankly alarming. McGovern's comments emphasised, however, what was already clear from the series itself: that according to the makers of *Banished* the central drama of Australia's colonisation was not the clash between European settlers and Indigenous peoples, but the clash between convicts and colonial authorities.

To this end, *Banished* puts the brutality and injustice of the British penal system on full display. The key challenge of the settlement at Sydney Cove, as depicted in this series, was the creation of a

---

16 Jimmy McGovern, 'BBC's Banished: How I Tried and Failed to get Indigenous Characters on TV', *Sydney Morning Herald*, 18 June 2015, accessed 3 November 2015, www.smh.com.au/entertainment/tv-and-radio/bbcs-banished-how-i-tried-and-failed-to-get-indigenous-characters-on-tv-20150618-ghrj3f.html.

17 Troy Bramston, 'BBC's Historical Whitewash Banishes Those Who Were Here Way Before Phillip', *The Australian*, 20 June 2015, p.3.

18 Bramston, 'BBC's Historical Whitewash'; Daley, '*Banished* Review'.

governable colony. This was achieved in part through sexual slavery: *Banished* discourages rebellion amongst the soldiers by assigning each one a female convict. Equally important for the control of the colony is the control of the convicts themselves, particularly the series' three main protagonists: Freeman, Tommy Barrett (Julian Rhind-Tutt) and Barrett's wife Elizabeth Quinn (MyAnna Buring). These three continually refuse the brutality and arbitrariness of colonial authority in the settlement by challenging those in positions of power. Their refusals are ultimately to no avail, and the possibility of rebellion is violently foreclosed by the hanging of Barrett at the hands of Freeman. This dramatic conclusion to the series marks the reassertion of colonial authority over the convict population.

Banished has the feel of a production from a different time: a kind of *Fatal Shore* meets *Damned Whores and God's Police* take on Australia's colonisation.[19] In this as much as anything else it is in sharp contrast to *The Secret River*, which suggests more recent historical influences.[20] It is also more difficult to take *Banished* seriously as historical television. There are only so many heightened evasions of the scaffold one series can take, and the constant use of the beach as the setting for scenes of drama or poignancy – it is even the location of the colony's graveyard – makes good actor Rhind-Tutt's description of *Banished* as "*Home and Away* on acid".[21] And yet, when watching it alongside *The Secret River*, I was most struck by their similarities. Both are interested in Australia's colonial beginnings, which they characterise as brutal, cruel, and unforgiving. Both pursue this past

---

19 Robert Hughes, *The Fatal Shore: A History of the Transportation of Convicts to Australia, 1787–1868*, Collins Harvill, London, 1987; Anne Summers, *Damned Whores and God's Police*, Penguin, Melbourne, 1975.

20 See for example Inga Clendinnen, *Dancing with Strangers: Europeans and Australians at First Contact*, Text, Melbourne, 2003; Grace Karskens, *The Colony: A History of Early Sydney*, Allen & Unwin, Sydney, 2009.

21 Julian Rhind-Tutt, cited in Graeme Blundell, 'Foundation of Fear', 20 June 2015, p.23.

through fictional means in ways that are likely to invite historians' displeasure. And both narrate their pasts in similar ways. In their understandings of Indigenous peoples, their developments of key romantic relationships, and their characterisations of white male settlers, *Banished* and *The Secret River* are not so different after all.

The lack of Indigenous characters in *Banished* does not translate into a complete erasure of Indigenous presence, and the way in which the series represents Indigeneity is revealing.[22] Almost all the series' main characters mention "the natives", and contact and conflict with Indigenous peoples is an imagined experience of the penal colony. The vicious and damaged Private Buckley (Adam Nagaitis), for example, expected the colony to be "Native women, all naked, all carrying armfuls of fruit, all wanting to fuck me". More typically Indigenous peoples are something to be feared. As Phillip explains in the first and last episode of the series, part of the role of the soldiers is to protect the colony from the threat of Indigenous attack. Yet the soldiers themselves are reluctant to chase after the absconding Freeman precisely because of their own fears. The death of a soldier from snakebite – the implausible result of running rather than walking through the bush – is explained in a letter home as a heroic death during an Indigenous attack. This fabricated attack is one of many scenes where the absence of Indigenous characters is at its most jarring. Even so, it does make clear that Indigenous peoples are a spectre for administrators, soldiers and convicts alike.

---

22 For discussions of the representation of Indigeneity on Australian television see: Marcia Langton, *'Well, I Heard it on the Radio and I Saw it on the Television': An Essay for the Australian Film Commission on the Politics and Aesthetics of Filmmaking by and about Aboriginal People and Things*, Australian Film Commission, Sydney, 1993; Frances Peters-Little, '"Nobles and Savages" on Television', *Aboriginal History* 27, 2003, pp.16–38; Michelle Arrow, '"History Should Not Have Ever Been How it Was": *The Colony*, *Outback House*, and Australian History', *Film and History* Vol. 37, No. 1, 2007, pp.54–66.

This representation is surprisingly similar to that of *The Secret River*, where Indigenous peoples are a threatening and worrying presence. When they first arrive at Thornhill's Point, the Thornhill children wonder whether "the blacks" will eat them. The family's first encounter is an unsettling scene of danger: five Dharug men arrive at the Point wielding spears and accompanied only by the sound of the bush. The sense of menace is compounded not long after by the murderous Smasher Sullivan (Tim Minchin):

> There are all sorts of stories up and down the river about their mischief. Scalped two men alive by South Creek. Took a child out of its cradle, slit its little throat and sucked it dry up at Greenhills.

Perhaps adding to the fearful atmosphere is the sense that Indigenous peoples might not be the inferior "savages" *The Secret River*'s settlers had imagined. When the Thornhills clear land to plant their crop they clear away Dharug plantings of "yams". This disruption explains the initial hostility of the local peoples, but also characterises them as farmers, which is reinforced by the sympathetic Thomas Blackwood's (Lachy Hulme) explanation of their "clever" version of hunting using fire. Sal notices Indigenous women at their camp sweeping and weaving "just like we did back home", and explains to Will that "they're just like us". Medicine provided by an Indigenous woman saves Sal from "the fever". The local Dharug men are better able to make fire, to mimic Will's speech, and to trade with the Thornhills to their advantage. And the local peoples' relationship with the land trumps even Will's desires: "It's theirs Will", Sal says after a Dharug group led by Greybeard/Gumang (Trevor Jamieson) set fire to the corn, "always 'as been. That's why they come and go, they've been doing it forever".

A similar sensibility can be found in *Banished*, albeit in less detail. The unseen "natives" are to blame for the shredding of the colony's fishing nets, a destructive but effective attempt to safeguard their own food supply. More interesting is Freeman's encounter with another absconder, Jefferson (Tim McCunn). Freeman flees the colony to escape punishment for the murder of another convict. He comes across Jefferson alone in the bush. It is a scene where the absence of Indigenous characters borders on bizarre: it's clear local peoples have helped Jefferson to survive, but it is only Jefferson we see. Jefferson is unexpectedly hostile to Freeman, and as he gives chase he explains Indigenous hunting practices: "Freeman! I will smoke you out, that's how the natives catch a kangaroo. They set the bush alight, kangaroo comes running from the fire, straight on the native's spear".

The treatment of Indigenous Australia in *Banished* is more elision than erasure, and occasional references to the 'natives' make their absence more rather than less visible. One of the effects of the lack of characters, however, is to render Indigenous peoples as inscrutable, as beyond the understanding either of the series or of its protagonists. Something very similar happens in *The Secret River*, even with its different dramatic focus. Indigenous characters talk almost exclusively in language, and their behaviour and intention is often inferred rather than explained. They frequently walk through scenes without any reference to the Thornhills, who they look through as if they are not even there. Even when Will confronts a group of Dharug who have taken his corn – Will enraged, shotgun at his side, improbably explaining the inevitability of colonisation – the group only pauses briefly before continuing along their way. Indigenous peoples might be a larger feature of *The Secret River*, but in a way their lives and experiences are no more comprehensible than they are in *Banished*. In both series, it is the everyday lives and struggles of settlers that are the main focus.

This is in no way surprising: although there are clear differences in the dramatisation of colonisation in *The Secret River* and *Banished*, both are most interested in the European experience, and particularly in the experience of the transported. Strong romantic relationships between the main characters are key to their depictions of everyday life. In both productions these relationships are foundational, influencing storylines and driving character development. Watching as an historian they are distractingly contemporary, with the characteristics often associated with romantic relationships at the turn of the twenty-first century: they are exclusive, erotic, overwhelming, and transformative.[23] Researchers sometimes characterise the romantic ideal encoded in this twenty-first century relationship as in excess, and they worry about the implications of such high expectations for romantic love.[24] But in the worlds of *Banished* and *The Secret River* these relationships are essential to life in colonial New South Wales.

It makes sense, then, that there is an intensity to the romantic relationships of both *The Secret River* and *Banished*. In each production romantic partners are devoted to one another, although in *The Secret River* this devotion plays out with a little more subtlety. The Thornhills are equal partners who are affectionate, playful, loving, argumentative, and content. The miniseries opens with their arrival at Sydney Cove. As a dishevelled Will is rowed ashore, Sal can be heard yelling his name from another longboat. Once on the beach she forces her way towards him in desperation. When she reaches him her purpose becomes clear: she has found a way to have Will assigned to her. Later we learn that Sal was responsible for the conversion of Will's sentence from death to transportation. Will's feelings for Sal sometimes seem a little less passionately felt in comparison, but even so they are a strong presence. When Sal is ill with a "fever", for example, Will sends his

---

23 For a consideration of contemporary romantic love see for example William Jankowiak and Thomas Palladino, eds, *Intimacies: Love and Sex Across Cultures*, Columbia University Press, New York, 2008; and Mary Evans, *Love: An Unromantic Discussion*, Polity, Cambridge, 2003.

24 See William Reddy, *The Making of Romantic Love: Longing and Sexuality in Europe, South Asia, and Japan, 900–1200 CE*, The University of Chicago Press, 2012, 382–83.

eldest son Willie (Rory Potter) off for help while he stays behind to nurse her, turning to prayer in his desperation to keep her alive. Even Will's involvement in *The Secret River*'s massacre, which poisons his relationship with his other son Dickie (Finn Scicluna-O'Prey), cannot undo their bond: the miniseries ends with them in later years, distant but still affectionate, reminiscing about London.

The romantic relationships of *Banished* are similarly intense, although the consequences of this intensity are more melodramatically felt. The series begins and ends with the relationship between Barrett and Quinn. Barrett is dangerously devoted to Quinn. From the very first episode it is clear that he is willing – even eager – to hang for her. He is fiercely and murderously protective of her as a result: he strangles the unpopular convict Marston (Rory McCann) in a rage at Marston's treatment of her, and viciously attacks Private Buckley after realising he and Quinn had a sexual liaison. Barrett's attack on Buckley leads him to the scaffold, where he refuses a hood "because I wanted your face to be the last thing I saw, the face I loved more than anything else in the world". Quinn's love for Barrett is less dangerous, but no less intense. She trades sexual favours with Buckley precisely to try to protect Barrett from punishment for their clandestine relationship. And she distracts him from his impending death with professions of love of his bravery, strength, shrewdness, kindness, and sexual prowess.

In spite of its primacy to the series, the basis of the romantic connection between Barrett and Quinn is not really explained. But the basis of other relationships is explained through intimate conversation. All of the romantic relationships in *Banished* are developed and fostered through conversation, often in bed and after dark. This is particularly true of the relationships between Major Ross, Corporal MacDonald (Ryan Corr), and the convict Katherine McVitie (Joanna Vanderham). Their love triangle is melodramatic historical romance at its swashbuckling finest. McVitie is assigned to MacDonald in the colony's initial sexual barter. As Ross discovers, however, McVitie and MacDonald conspired to ensure they were together. Ross uses this information to force MacDonald to "share" McVitie with him. McVitie insists they have no option but to abide by Ross' request, and she comforts MacDonald by insisting that Ross will "not have my mind, nor my heart". But when Ross offers McVitie conversation and companionship rather than sex – "fully dressed" – only MacDonald can see the danger: "I would sooner you fuck him than talk to him", he says. All the intimate "fully dressed" talking leads inevitably back to sex, and McVitie leaves MacDonald for Ross.

The importance of intimate conversation to romantic relationships is similarly emphasised in *The Secret River*. Will and Sal talk everything through, and again this often takes place in bed at the end of the day. Many of their conversations are disagreements: over returning home, or moving to the Hawkesbury, or their business plans, or, much later, Sal's unwillingness to remain at Thornhill's Point as the conflict with the Dharug heightens. After Smasher Sullivan's violence towards the local peoples becomes clear to them, they even discuss the prospect of Will's involvement in actions against them: "Promise me Will you won't never do anything like that", she says. Will breaks this promise, and his part in the massacre is one of the few things they don't discuss openly: Will denies his involvement, though it's clear Sal doesn't believe him.

The difficulties of that conversation is one of several ways *The Secret River* makes clear that Will's participation in violence against Indigenous peoples is not by choice. The miniseries explains Will's involvement in terms of the Dharug people's disruptive behaviour, which slowly fuels his anger. Even so, Will acts only after the spearing death of the disturbed and bereaved Saggity (Samuel Johnson). He questions the ringleader Smasher Sullivan's plans for a surprise attack. And he is a deeply reluctant participant, hanging back from the violence. For the most part Will is more observer than perpetrator, shooting only when prompted or threatened. Back at Thornhill's Point he is deeply traumatised as he washes blood from his shirt, seen only by Dickie. He presses a bloodied finger to his lips and implores his son to keep the difficult secret. Will is the violent white settler as we would perhaps like to imagine him in 2015 Australia: reluctant, ashamed, damaged, and with a deep if hidden sense of the implications of his actions.

Although the violence is directed elsewhere, a similar move is at play in *Banished*: the participation of settlers in violence is the result of a lack of alternatives. There are several examples of this throughout the series, from governor to convict, but the most dramatic can be seen in Freeman's hanging of Barrett, his closest friend and ally. Freeman is manipulated by Phillip into becoming the colony's hangman: he can either be hanged for the murder of Marston, or he can hang the next convict to transgress. "What would you do to live", Phillip asks Freeman as he is on the scaffold, noose around his neck, last rights in the background. "Would you be our hangman?" Freeman agrees through stereotypically gritted teeth. When it becomes clear that the first to be hanged will be Barrett, he contemplates hanging himself instead, standing once again on the scaffold with the noose around his neck and his hand on the trapdoor lever. But he cannot do it; as he explains to Barrett, "I loved you Tommy, but I loved life more". Like Thornhill, his part in this violence is under duress. Freeman is another violent white (convict) settler as we might like to see him in 2015: remorseful, saddened, and determined to make amends. Both *Banished* and *The Secret River* continue a long-standing trend of narrating the white settler as victim.[25]

Of course, the circumstances of settler violence in *Banished* and *The Secret River* are very different, and I don't want to simply conflate them. But the lack of alternatives afforded to settlers enacting violence

---

25 See Ann Curthoys, 'Expulsion, Exodus and Exile in White Australian Historical Mythology', *Journal of Australian Studies* No. 61, 1999, pp.1–18.

unfolds in similar ways. In both productions foundational violence is not really the fault of the individual, but is driven by forces beyond his control – the profound unfairness of British society at the turn of the nineteenth century, for example, or the depravities of the penal system. Although the structural causes of violence are important, in this case they are a deeply unsatisfying explanation because they allow the violent protagonists of *The Secret River* and *Banished* a free pass. This might be a very familiar dramatisation of Australia's colonisation, but it is not a particularly productive one.

It is difficult for us to really know what convict settlers in colonial New South Wales considered to be the central drama of the creation of the colony. Although *Banished* and *The Secret River* offer contrasting interpretations – in one it is the conflict between convicts and colonial authorities, in the other it is the conflict between settlers and Indigenous peoples – the way they do so is surprisingly similar, as this chapter has mapped out. In the long run it's likely that *The Secret River* will outshine *Banished*. This is not necessarily because it is more 'accurate', but rather because it speaks more directly to the historical concerns of contemporary Australia, engaging with a past that has been the subject of considerable public debate for more than two decades. If that is indeed the case, I can only hope that the self-congratulatory impulse that seems to surround all the incarnations of *The Secret River* doesn't distract from the need for careful and considered analysis of the strategies and politics of this text.

CHAPTER 12

Struggle Street ... Poverty Porn?

ZORA SIMIC

"There are a lot of people who come from Mount Druitt who end up becoming really successful mate", says a scruffy local in the opening moments of *Struggle Street*, the three-hour observational documentary series that aired on SBS in May 2015. The viewer did not meet these people nor did we enter their homes. Instead, guided by a cliché-ridden narration provided by actor David Field at his most over-the-top laconic, we met a purposefully selected group of public housing tenants whose lives epitomise the problems that disproportionately plague Australia's underclass: welfare dependence, unemployment, drug addiction, intergenerational poverty, family violence, crime, homelessness and poor mental and/ or physical health, to name the more obvious ones.

Two of the 'stars' of the show – ice addict Corey Kennedy, who stole from his own dad to feed his habit, and Billie Joe Wilkie, filmed smoking a bong with her mum while heavily pregnant – provided the most tut-tutting opportunities for the commentariat and ensured it was not necessary to have watched the show beyond these allegedly emblematic moments to have a very strong opinion about it. Billie Joe in particular incurred the wrath of an otherwise unlikely coalition of right-wing old men and the prominent blogger Mia Freedman, who then applauded social services for taking the baby (her third) away.[1]

---

1   Mia Freedman, 'The biggest problem with the pregnant bong scene on Struggle Street', *Mamamia*, 14 May 2015, www.mamamia.com.au/parenting/billie-jo-on-struggle-street/.

Struggle Street was controversial before the first episode even aired thanks to a bombastic promotional advertisement so overflowing with stereotypes about a divided Sydney – postcard beaches and glamorous denizens in the east, police sirens and dysfunctional inhabitants in the west – it was clearly designed to provoke both outrage and interest. And so it came to pass. The Mayor of Blacktown Stephen Bali led the charge with his accusation that *Struggle Street* was nothing more than "publicly funded poverty porn".[2] He demanded SBS pull the promo and the entire series from the air, approached then-Communications Minister Malcolm Turnbull to do so, started an online petition at change.org in which, on behalf of some of the participants of the show, he accused the producers of unethical conduct, and led a highly publicised garbage truck protest outside SBS headquarters. As a "gesture of goodwill", SBS arranged for the advertisement to be pulled from the schedule, but not even the threat of a defamation case stopped the show from going on.[3] The first episode attracted a whopping 1.31 million viewers, easily winning the timeslot everywhere, and giving SBS its highest ratings since the 2014 Football World Cup.[4]

By sheer volume of media commentary, *Struggle Street* went head-to-head with the likes of *The Bachelor*, while easily surpassing its commercial rivals in terms of the range of opinions on offer. Seasoned opinion writers, serious and tabloid journalists, past and present residents, state and federal politicians and thousands of others on

2 'Struggle Street: garbage truck protest against SBS "poverty porn" documentary, *ABC News*, 6 May 2015, www.abc.net.au/news/2015-05-06/garbage-truck-protest-again-sbs-reality-tv-struggle-street/6448012.

3 Georgina Mitchell, 'Struggle Street backlash: SBS pulls promo advertisement', *Sydney Morning Herald*, 2 May 2015, www.smh.com.au/entertainment/tv-and-radio/struggle-street-backlash-sbs-pulls-promo-advertisement-20150502-1myi9j.html.

4 Michael Lallo, 'Struggle Street sets record ratings for an SBS documentary, with 1.31 million viewers', *Sydney Morning Herald*, 7 May 2015, www.smh.com.au/entertainment/tv-and-radio/struggle-street-sets-ratings-record-for-an-sbs-documentary-with-131-million-viewers 20150507-ggw15r.html.

social media offered their views on whether or not they agreed with Mayor Bali's 'poverty porn' assessment.

At one extreme, tabloid newspaper *The Daily Telegraph*, in an audacious feat of hypocrisy, considering their own history of targeting 'dole bludgers' and 'welfare cheats', (especially those from Western Sydney) to sell papers, revealed financial and personal details about Leonie Lowe, head of KEO Films Australia, producers of the series, and SBS Managing Director Michael Ebeid (including about his "younger boyfriend"). This was presumably to demonstrate how these Darlinghurst dwellers on "easy street" each profited from 'porn' at the expense of the poor and the taxpayers of Australia.[5]

At the other end, many critics and viewers responded positively to the first episode, assessing it as essential and sobering viewing about an oft-neglected segment of Australian society. The word 'resilience' popped up a lot to describe the people in the show and at the hashtag #strugglestreet, some viewers asked how they could help assist the service providers in the area.[6] Cultural critic Steve Dow expressed in his review of the first episode what became a common response: the "misjudged promo moment", with its sneering snippets of local colour, including one of the participants farting on his verandah, did not do justice to the "extraordinary group of subjects" profiled.[7] Dow's condemnation of the heavy-handed narration was also widely shared, by opponents and supporters alike.

5   Janet Fife-Yeomans and Miles Godfrey, 'Struggle Street: SBS Chief Michael Ebeid lives a very different life to those profiled by the controversial series', *The Daily Telegraph*, 6 May 2015, www.dailytelegraph.com.au/news/nsw/struggle-street-sbs-chief-michael-ebeid-lives-a-very-different-life-to-those-profiled-by-the-controversial-series/story-fnpn118l-1227337806615.

6   Caroline Overington, 'Important viewing or Poverty Porn? Struggle Street surprises viewers', *The Australian Women's Weekly*, 7 May 2015, www.aww.com.au/latest-news/news-stories/morning-news-wrap-may-7-20480.

7   Steve Dow, 'Struggle Street review – must-see TV, undersold by sensationalism', *The Guardian*, 6 May 2015, www.theguardian.com/tv-and-radio/2015/may/06/struggle-street-review-must-see-tv-undersold-by-sensationalism.

The term 'poverty porn' has been around for some decades now, but as this sample of commentary demonstrates, it was *Struggle Street* that brought it into mainstream conversation in Australia. Given this, and also Mount Druitt's own special place in the history of representing disadvantage in Australia, *Struggle Street* – its genesis, content and reception – offers an ideal case study through which to ponder 'poverty porn'. What work does the category do as a form of critique? Has it become lazy shorthand? Does it expand or short-circuit analysis? There is no consensus about the term 'poverty porn' nor is there an authoritative definition or key theorist. It is an evolving critique that picks up all sorts of new criteria and inflections along the way. For Mayor Bali, for example, it was the publicly funded nature of *Struggle Street* that especially irked – surely public money would be better off assisting the poor rather than lampooning them on television? Many others agreed, as *Struggle Street* was singled out as the latest and most odious iteration of SBS's populist turn. I will return to these questions, but first let's consider the case for and against *Struggle Street* as poverty porn, including a recap of its alleged pornographic features.

"That's how some folks do it in the Druitt", drawled Field in the opening episode, as the cameras panned over neglected front lawns, graffiti-lashed buildings and public spaces full of the jobless or underemployed, idling about because there's nothing better to do. This is not the Sydney "in the tourist brochures", life is often a "dead-set struggle" and lives move "two steps forward and one step back".

At the heart of the series are the blended Kennedy family. Father Ashley is a former truckie on the disability pension after many health crises and his loving wife Peta has quit her good job to look after him. Between them, they have ten adult children, seven on the dole, including Tristan who has never properly recovered from a brain injury acquired in a motorbike accident, teenager Chloe who has epilepsy and Asperger's and has been so bullied it has led to suicidal thoughts, and Corey who is "on the ice". There are eighteen grandchildren, including Corey's toddler son Liam with girlfriend Shantelle. During the course of the series – filmed over six months – Corey descends deeper into addiction, steals from and fights with his dad, Ashley's sister dies before her time and much to Peta's despair, Ashley is diagnosed with early stage dementia.

However, not all is grim for the Kennedys: throughout, the family remain loving, with Ashley and Peta taking in Shantelle and Liam when Corey's drug use becomes intolerable. Tristan returns to Mount Druitt High to caution students about the dangers of driving without a helmet and manages to find a part time job, while Chloe receives an apology from one of her former bullies and together they turn her ordeal into a rap song.

In the first episode Ashley and his mate Tony, AKA 'The Wog', are depicted scrounging for scraps in the local streets and then blowing most of their earnings, sixty dollars, on a junk food binge in Seven Eleven – or so it seemed. Ashley, in one of a series of widely publicised corrections, later told the press he kept his money for essentials for his large family and it was the camera crew who paid for the meat pies.[8]

Shortly after that episode screened, Peta told women's magazine *New Idea* that the show "totally and cruelly humiliated my husband" and "caused so much heartache and drama ... we had no idea we were going to be portrayed this way".[9] By the third episode – in

---

8   Jane Bowron, 'Hard Lives and Blurred Truths in Struggle Street', www.stuff. co.nz, 28 August 2015, www.stuff.co.nz/entertainment/71536336/Review-Hard-lives-and-blurred-truths-in-Struggle-Street.

9   'Struggle Street Mum Peta Kennedy says SBS documentary "has ripped us apart"', www.newscom.au, May 11 2015, www.news.com.au/entertainment/tv/reality-tv/struggle-street-mum-peta-kennedy-says-sbs-documentary-has-ripped-us-apart/news-story/b73ac50de773884c7591b4db835d3adf.

which Chloe performed her rap song – Peta spoke more positively to the press about the series and hoped the episode sent out a strong anti-bullying message.[10]

We also follow scrappy sixteen-year old Bailee, transient since age 13, after her stepfather violently attacked her and her mum threw her out. Bailee, we soon discover, has also been raped, has a history of depression, self-harm and drug abuse and was only recently released from a stint in hospital. From this rock bottom, Bailee picks herself up, with a little help from a new friend. She is offered counsel and shelter by take-charge Erin, a young single mum who accompanies Bailee to her last residence, a shit-sauce-urine stained Housing Commission townhouse to pick up her things.

Their blossoming friendship is warmly portrayed and some critics singled out Erin as an especially inspiring figure. Still, Erin accused the producers of misleading her about the style of documentary – when first approached in a local park she was told the creators hoped to counter Mount Druitt's 'bad name' – and labelled the outcome "disgusting".[11] When lawyers from high-profile legal firm Shine offered to represent some of the residents pro bono in a defamation suit against SBS, it was the producers' alleged breach of 'duty of care' obligations to underage Bailee that they singled out for special attention.[12]

---

10 Alison Balding and Danielle Jarvis, 'Strong Anti-Bully message emerges from SBS's Struggle Street', 15 May 2015, www.dailytelegraph.com.au/newslocal/west/strong-anti-bully-message-emerges-from-sbss-struggle-street/story-fngr8i5s-1227355278836.

11 Alison Balding, 'Struggle Street stars prepare for show's final instalment', 13 May 2015, www.heraldsun.com.au/newslocal/west/struggle-street-stars-prepare-for-shows-final-instalment/story-fngr8i5s-1227352199055.

12 Taylor Auerbach, 'Struggle Street: Featured Western Sydney locals set to sue SBS over their portrayal', 8 May 2015, www.dailytelegraph.com.au/news/nsw/struggle-street-featured-western-sydney-locals-set-to-sue-sbs-over-their-portrayal/story-fni0cx12-1227344685802.

William, an Aboriginal man who has lived in Mount Druitt for over twenty-five years, is also homeless when first introduced. No longer welcome with his mob in the area, he's getting by with his sling shot skills and sleeping rough on the rural fringes. When William shares his recipe for cooking up birds in an Italian sauce, he provides a straightforward set of instructions that were nonetheless subtitled, as if in a curious mash up of cooking show and anthropological documentary. Estranged from his two sons, William represents himself as a man caught between two cultures and speculates he may have been better off before invasion. William has no identification and as his story develops, he applies for his birth certificate so that he can find his mother. For former New South Wales Labor Premier and life-long 'westie' Nathan Rees, one of several commentators with 'insider' knowledge who praised the series during its short season, "intrepid" and "resilient" William's story was an especially "poignant" one.[13]

By episodes two and three, Rees had far less patience for 47 year-old Bob, one time heroin addict and recent ice user, and his much younger girlfriend Billie Jo, pregnant with her third child. Initially the viewer – not to mention Bob – assumes it's his baby. Later we're not so sure. By the time Billie Jo goes into premature labour, smoking a cigarette to take the edge off the pain, we've already seen her and Bob trying to break into a housemate's room to find a missing piece for their bong and of course "the Horrifying Scene that shocked Australia!", to quote the website of 2Day FM.[14] In a scene destined to go down in observational documentary history, Billie Jo sits on the toilet toting on her home made bong while her mum Carline counsels her about quitting ice and "only smoking cones from now on" for the

---

13   Nathan Rees, 'Education is the key to turning Struggle Street around', *The Drum*, 18 May 2015, www.abc.net.au/news/2015-05-14/rees-education-is-the-key-to-turning-struggle-street-around/6469778.

14   We Guy Josh, 'The Horrifying Scene that Shocked Australia!', 14 May 2015, www.2dayfm.com.au/scoopla/tv/blog/2015/5/the-horrifying-struggle-street-scene-that-shocked-australia/.

sake of the baby. We've also learned that Billie Jo was born addicted to methadone, that her brother died of a drug overdose, her sister of motor neurone disease at age 30, that her father is a schizophrenic and that Bob has a tragic backstory too: his wife Caron has been living in a nursing home since suffering an aneurysm. Billie Jo's baby boy, like his two siblings, is taken into care shortly after he's born.

By the time the 'bong' episode aired, Billie Jo's mum had left the family for another man and Billie Jo was in remand for shoplifting and driving charges and for missing multiple court appearances. The Australian edition of the salacious British tabloid *The Daily Mail*, a long-time purveyor of poverty porn, relayed the details of Billie Jo's imprisonment in faux-sympathetic detail in a series of features saturated with negative images of Mount Druitt. Because of her notoriety, reported the *Daily Mail*, Billie Jo was locked up in the segregation section of Silverwater Women's Correctional Centre with some of the "worst female murderers and baby killers" in Australia.[15] In an interview with Billie Jo, the reporter also assured readers that the *Daily Mail* offered no payment to her other than a McDonalds' meal she had requested.[16]

The final story arc in *Struggle Street* was a more promising one. Perennial foster kid Chris, now in his twenties, was living with his aunt, had finally managed to land a regular job, as a cleaner in a rugby league club, and had reunited his aunt with her twin, his mentally ill mum. Chris' struggles had hardly stopped altogether;

---

15   Candace Sutton and Heather McNab, 'From Struggle Street to Australia's Toughest Female Prison', 19 May 2015, www.dailymail.co.uk/news/article-3087322/Bong-smoking-mother-shocked-Struggle-Street-viewers-locked-murderers-baby-killers-Australias-toughest-womens-prison.html.

16   Candace Sutton, Sally Lee and Emily Crane, 'Born addicted to methadone', *The Daily Mail*, 6 May 2015, www.dailymail.co.uk/news/article-3069673/Born-addicted-methadone-tragic-life-star-Struggle-Street-filmed-taking-drugs-pregnant-revealed-released-jail-just-time-watch-troubling-story-unfold-screen.html.

after all he suffers from at least a handful of mental health issues and daily endures lengthy commutes to get to his low paid job, a familiar grind for outer suburban workers. But he tries and, after the bong scene generated a second wave of backlash against the series, many viewers and critics latched onto Chris as an exemplar of self-care and improvement.

These affirmations for Chris' great strides, coupled with the vitriolic blasts against Billie Jo, fall into the 'deserving versus undeserving poor' paradigm. They also fuelled the arguments of opponents to the *Struggle Street* approach to representing poverty, whereby overcoming it is an individual triumph or failing and little effort is made to understand disadvantage at a deeper, structural level. *Struggle Street*, wrote El Gibbs in *Overland*, "is without context, leaving particular families to wear the blame for being poor".[17] Gibbs, like others concerned *Struggle Street* trivialised rather than illuminated poverty, buttressed her critique with details from the Australian Council of Social Services' (ACOSS) 2014 *Poverty in Australia* report. This strategy was also employed by Federal Shadow Assistant Treasurer Dr Andrew Leigh, who tried to re-direct the debate away from the charge of poverty porn to the bare facts of "deep and entrenched poverty in a prosperous country".[18]

However, while *Struggle Street* provided some hook and colour to otherwise statistic-laden reports buried in corners of newspapers, and new material for regular spokespeople on inequality in Australia such as Senator Leigh, more immediately confronting for most were the actual people on the screen. Did they properly 'represent' Mount Druitt? Did they consent and if so under what terms? What were

17 El Gibbs, 'Struggling with the Facts', *Overland*, 12 May 2015, https://overland. org.au/2015/05/struggling-with-the-facts/.

18 Gareth Hutchins, 'SBS's Struggle Street controversy missed the point, says Labor frontbencher', 20 May 2015, www.smh.com.au/federal-politics/political-news/ sbss-struggle-street-controversy-missed-the-point-says-labor-frontbencher-20150520-gh5ljl.html.

the ethical obligations of the producers? Is the viewer a voyeur for devouring this as entertainment? In other words, is *Struggle Street* poverty porn?

The advertisement for *Struggle Street* was definitely poverty porn, said nearly every commentator: it sensationalised the lives of Mount Druitt locals to the point of ridicule to entice people to watch. It upset some of the participants, who claimed to have been misled and misrepresented. So far, so very poverty porn, but for some the series itself was a trickier proposition. As discussed, once the whole series went to air, or at least the first episode, many viewers were drawn in by the people on the screen and their stories and the cheap tricks of the promo were forgiven or at least dismissed as a badly pitched or deceptive stunt. Consensus around what poverty porn is broke down and more often than not the use of the term was qualified.

For *The Guardian's* Gay Alcorn, the onus was on the viewer: *Struggle Street* would only become poverty porn "if we have a look, kind of enjoy being sad and shocked, and then turn away to other things". As a journalist, she confessed that poverty in its humdrum statistical detail – 2.5 million Australians live below the poverty line, according to welfare groups – does not make for an interesting story. *Struggle Street* manages to shock because it pushes "what being marginalised feels like … in our faces".[19]

Jane Goodall, TV writer for *Inside Story*, also stopped short of the poverty porn label, but questioned the motivations of the series' creators rather than its viewers. She detailed a whole list of serious ethical problems, from not giving participants an opportunity to

---

19 Gay Alcorn, 'Struggle Street is only poverty porn if we enjoy watching then turn away', 15 May 2015, www.theguardian.com/commentisfree/2015/may/15/struggle-street-is-only-poverty-porn-if-we-enjoy-watching-then-turn-away.

preview and endorse how they were represented to manipulative editing techniques to issues of informed consent from vulnerable people, including minors who had recently attempted suicide (Bailee) or were suffering from cognitive impairment (Tristan). The subjects of *Struggle Street* and similar series, wrote Goodall, are unpaid labour feeding the profits of international media corporations.[20] On these last grounds Goodall's critique supports academic Steven Threadgold's definition of poverty porn as producing "abjectifying images of the poor through a privileged gaze for privileged gratification".[21]

As Threadgold's definition highlights, exploitation of the poor for the purposes of profit and/ or entertainment – which may be well intentioned or at least presented that way – is what is said to mark out some representations of poverty as pornographic. Using this basic criterion, critics have traced a poverty porn tradition, dating back to the 1980s and the widespread use of images of starving African children with swollen bellies to generate sympathy (and donations) in the developed world for victims of Third World famine. More recently, the 2009 Oscar-winning film *Slumdog Millionaire* has been accused of trivialising life in India's slums to make a feel-good box office hit, while a whole glut of post global financial crisis TV shows focusing on poor parts of Britain and the United States have been lambasted as patronising and as misleadingly badged as documentaries rather than the less noble genre of reality television.

Across all of these examples, poverty porn is identified as much by what it does not do as what it does: World Vision campaigns represent Africa monolithically and its inhabitants as poor, suffering victims with famine as a calamity that has befallen the region, much like a natural disaster, rather than the outcome of global geo-politics

---

20 Jane Goodall, 'An Ethical Tightrope Across Struggle Street', 8 May 2015, http:// insidestory.org.au/an-ethical-tightrope-across-struggle-street.

21 Steven Threadgold, 'Struggle Street is Poverty Porn with an extra dose of class racism', 6 May 2015, http://theconversation.com/struggle-street-is-poverty-porn-with-an-extra-dose-of-class-racism-41346.

and western hegemony. *Slumdog Millionaire*, meanwhile, was accused
of recycling ancient stereotypes about India at the expense of proper
engagement with its postcolonial present – and even worse, the film
was directed by Danny Boyle: a white, British man.[22] As for the
likes of *Benefits Street*, the high-rating British documentary series
set in Birmingham that screened in the UK in early 2014, critics
have argued that the creators of such shows, which typically capture
the more sensationalised aspects of welfare dependence (one episode
featured a demonstration of how to shoplift), feed into the anti-welfare
campaigns of conservative governments rather than challenge them.
Indeed, *Benefits Street* was raised as evidence by Conservative MPs
in the House of Commons of the urgent need for welfare reform in
austerity Britain.

Using *Benefits Street* as an example, in an analysis pertinent to
Struggle Street, sociologist Tracey Jensen has argued that poverty porn
is now also a highly orchestrated media event that typically begins
with producers denying their work is any such thing, but is instead a
'raw' and 'honest' portrayal of a neglected segment of society. With
the terms of discourse thus established, poverty porn reproduces
itself in the hothouse of fast media. Under the auspices of 'debate',
the usual suspects and the occasional interloper – though rarely,
Jensen laments, any social scientists – "comment on representations
as if they were real".[23] Jensen sees no political utility in this cycle

22 *Slumdog Millionaire* has the most contested position in the poverty porn canon – it
is a fictional film, the producers have provided some monetary support to local
participants and it has been argued that its plucky child protagonists have far more
agency than the docile African children awaiting rescue in development porn.
For a comparative discussion of poverty porn see Matt Collin, 'What is "poverty
porn" and what does it mean for development?', *Aid Thoughts*, 1 July 2009, http://
aidthoughts.org/?p=69.

23 Tracey Jensen, 'Welfare Commonsense, Poverty Porn and Doxosophy', *Sociological
Research Online*, Vol. 19, No. 3, p.3, April 2014, www.socresonline.org.uk/19/3/3.
html DOI: 10.5153/sro.3441, 3.3.

whatsoever, except of course for politicians eager to appropriate poverty porn as fact.

Struggle Street certainly conformed to this template, at least in broad terms, and this was hardly surprising considering the producers. While only the second locally produced series for KEO Films Australia – the first was the thoroughly pleasant lifestyle series *River Cottage Australia* – their British parent company was responsible for *Skint*, a documentary series set in a housing estate in Scunthorpe, once a thriving industrial town and now full of the long-term unemployed, that first aired in Britain in 2013. The producers of *Skint* and *Struggle Street* made similar claims about their motivations – putting on screen the human faces and stories of "our most socially-disadvantaged communities"[24] – and each spent time in their chosen suburbs, establishing a feel for the place and most importantly finding locals "who had stories to tell".[25]

Like *Skint*, *Struggle Street* also featured an irritating voice-over, intergenerational welfare dependence and a pregnant young woman / new mother with drug problems whose behaviour was singled out for extra special scrutiny and judgement in the seemingly bottomless pit of divided commentary both series generated.

Yet while *Skint* and *Struggle Street* shared much in common in terms of content and as media event, it would sell any analysis of *Struggle Street* short to represent it as merely derivative of a British phenomenon. As media event, *Struggle Street* both expanded and narrowed definitions of poverty porn. The expansion came courtesy of closer inspection of this term and new criteria to either claim or disqualify *Struggle Street* from this genre. Yet as case study, *Struggle Street* was only occasionally referenced in relation to the recent poverty porn

---

24 www.keofilms.com.au/index/#/strugglestreet/.

25 Nigel F, 'Skint producer explains why they chose Scunthorpe', 20 May 2013, www.scunthorpetelegraph.co.uk/Skint-producer-explains-chose-Scunthorpe/ story-19020291-detail/story.html.

explosion on UK television or the longer history of the term. This is because the term poverty porn provided for some a pithy name to describe historic and enduring negative representations of Sydney's western suburbs and Mount Druitt in particular.

When Stephen Bali accused the creators of *Struggle Street* and SBS of peddling poverty porn he did so as the mayor of a region that has long been shorthand for disadvantage and dysfunction. In a debate with SBS content director Helen Kellie on ABC's *Lateline*, Bali said the show had left the people of Mount Druitt "devastated" and that it stigmatised the whole of Western Sydney – again. "This stereotype, we're over it and it shouldn't happen".[26]

Mount Druitt's notoriety in the national imaginary dates back to at least 1981 and the hyperbolic coverage of the 'Bidwell riot', that allegedly began when a fight between two female students from rival high schools attracted a tabloid-reported crowd of a thousand teenagers. The 'riot' was purportedly spurred along by enterprising journalists eager to generate a sensationalist story from a schoolyard brawl.[27]

In the mid-1990s, Mount Druitt's teenagers again attracted negative national attention when the *Daily Telegraph* ran a cover story, featuring school photographs of the entire year-twelve graduating class, under the headline 'The Class We Failed'. It is a story that has been revisited by other media outlets ever since, most recently

26 Lindy Kerin and Thuy Ong, 'Struggle Street: Mount Druitt community up in arms over 'poverty porn' documentary series on SBS', *ABC News* 6 May 2015, www.abc.net.au/news/2015-05-05/sbs-struggle-street-series-poverty-porn-says-mt-druitt-mayor/6446648.

27 Mark Peel, *The Lowest Rung: Voices of Australian Poverty*, Cambridge University Press, Melbourne, 2003, pp.17–21.

in coverage of the launch of the MySchool website that first made public school performance and rankings in 2010.[28]

Using the Bidwell example as paradigmatic, historian Mark Peel in his important study of poverty in Australia, *The Lowest Rung* (2003), traced how "poverty news and poverty knowledge", whether generated by "sojourning" journalists or social scientists, relies on an established repertoire of tropes that even when ostensibly well-intentioned have real-world and sometimes damaging effects.[29] In the immediate aftermath of the so-called riots, for instance, Mount Druitt residents were subject to increased bureaucratic surveillance, while negative stereotypes about Sydney's western suburbs were further entrenched. The stigma of coming from Mount Druitt has also been identified by some residents, including former students of the 'class that failed', as personally and professionally damaging.[30]

The flipside to this history of negative portrayals about Mount Druitt has been resistance, whether specifically targeted (in 1997, *The Daily Telegraph* were successfully sued for defamation) or through proud assertions of local or 'westie' identity. Among the creative responses to *Struggle Street* were the garbage truck workers who, according to Mayor Bali, put their hands up to protest at the 'garbage' on television and a YouTube series called Made in Mount Druitt comissioned by Street University, a program run by the Ted Noffs Foundation, and designed to celebrate local talent.

The media also had no trouble finding locals ready to criticise the slant of the documentary. Local TAFE students complained to *The Daily Telegraph* that *Struggle Street* showed all of the bad and little of

---

28 Jessica Mahar, 'Painful Memories of Mount Druitt's maligned class of '96', 29 January 2010, www.smh.com.au/national/education/painful-memories-of-mount-druitts-maligned-class-of-96-20100128-n1sd.html.

29 Peel, *The Lowest Rung*, p.16.

30 George Morgan, 'A Tale of Two Cities: Distinction, Dispersal and Disassociation in Western Sydney', in *After Sprawl: Post-Suburban Sydney: E-Proceedings of the 'Post-Suburban Sydney: The City in Transformation' Conference*, 2005, pp.1–9.

the good of Mount Druitt and "made everyone look like idiots",[31] while the audience special episode of *Q & A* was jam packed with locals and their advocates – including well-spoken high school students, exasperated service providers and of course Mayor Bali – highly critical of the series' all-too-familiar portrayal of their suburb. Here too the features of poverty porn were further elaborated. One of the panellists, playwright Nakkiah Lui, who grew up in Mount Druitt, while sympathetic to some aspects, argued that the team behind *Struggle Street* crossed the line into poverty porn by not allowing their subjects to actively participate in how their stories were told.[32]

Not all Mount Druitt locals – or westies or housing commission tenants or others with claims to insider knowledge – objected to *Struggle Street*. Declarations of recognition and emphatic endorsements of its authenticity were common among the thousands of online comments, as were second opinions and mixed feelings. Some of the team behind Street Uni's Made in Mount Druitt campaign for instance tempered their initial negative reactions to the promo once they saw the show.[33] The terms of the poverty porn debate work against such ambiguity and rely on the generation of strong emotions, but the effects are not always predictable or stable.

Over half a year later, the longer term consequences of *Struggle Street*'s ratings success are most apparent in the decision by SBS to commission another series in another poverty-stricken part of urban

31 Taylor Auerbach, 'Struggle Street: Featured Western Sydney Locals set to sue SBS over portrayal', 8 May 2015, www.dailytelegraph.com.au/news/nsw/struggle-street-featured-western-sydney-locals-set-to-sue-sbs-over-their-portrayal/story-fni0cx12-1227344685802.

32 Q & A: Struggle Street on Budget Eve, broadcast 11 May 2015, www.abc.net.au/tv/qanda/txt/s4212658.htm.

33 Nick Galvin, 'Struggle Street: DJ Zehrish Naera putting a fresh spin on Mount Druitt', 14 May 2015, www.smh.com.au/entertainment/tv-and-radio/struggle-street-dj-zehrish-naera-putting-a-fresh-spin-on-mount-druitt-20150514-gh1gcc.html.

Australia, thus emulating the *Once Upon A Time In* [a notorious multi-cultural suburb] format. Yet for a week or so back in May 2015, it seemed the series had pushed inequality and disadvantage to the centre of national conversation. In this regard, *Struggle Street* was *Zeitgeist* television, airing in the wake of the 2014 'lifters and leaners' Federal budget, widely regarded as the most inequitable in recent history, and in the midst of a purported ice epidemic and a verifiable housing crisis. *Struggle Street* addressed these issues, and more, but it did so in a sometimes exploitative fashion to a historically scapegoated community. By choosing Mount Druitt, the producers – the local branch of a production company at the vanguard of British poverty porn – knew exactly what they were doing.

As poverty porn, then, *Struggle Street* hit all its targets. It generated outrage, opposition and huge ratings. The creators, under the guise of myth busting, made over a million people watch and when we did many of us were compelled and even moved by what we saw. At its best, *Struggle Street* generated insight and empathy: an ice addict in the family could happen to any of us! At its worst, the producers piled up Billie Jo's transgressions and threw her to the wolves. As critique, poverty porn sometimes provided the perfect vocabulary to respond to all of this, but by encouraging commentators to declare their hand – *Struggle Street* is utter rubbish and SBS should be defunded or *Struggle Street* is not porn, it's 'real' – the charge left little room for ambivalence and uncertainty. Finally, as framework, poverty porn reminds us the Australian media still has no idea about how to manage or receive stories about the underclass. Observational documentary aims to humanise its subjects, but 'us' and 'them' remains the dominant mode of talking about poverty in Australia, no matter what the statistics are trying to tell us: inequality is growing and its right here.

About the Contributors

Michelle Arrow is Associate Professor in Modern History at Macquarie University. She is the author of numerous book chapters and articles on a wide range of topics, including the representation of history in the media, the sexual and cultural politics of the 1970s, and the history of popular culture. Her books include *Friday on Our Minds: Popular Culture in Australia since 1945* (2009) and, as co-editor, *The Chamberlain Case Reader* (2009). Michelle won the 2014 NSW Premier's Multimedia History Prize for the radio documentary 'Public Intimacies: the 1974–1977 Royal Commission on Human Relationships'. In 2016, Michelle held a National Library of Australia Fellowship, researching a feminist history of the 1970s in Australia.

Jeannine Baker is a historian and documentary maker in the Department of Media, Music, Communication and Cultural Studies at Macquarie University. She is the author of *Australian Women War Reporters: Boer War to Vietnam* (NewSouth, 2015). Her most recent radio documentary is *Holding a Tiger by the Tail: Jessie Litchfield* (2015).

Dr Liz Giuffre is a Lecturer in Communication at the University of Technology Sydney, as well as a freelance arts journalist. Her interests include popular music studies, screen studies, genre (especially comedy) and audience studies.

Dr Mark Hearn is a lecturer in the Department of Modern History and Politics, Macquarie University. He has published widely in the field of Australian history and contributed a number of opinion pieces on Australian politics and history in the mainstream press. He was the co-editor of *Rethinking Work: Time Space Discourse*, published by Cambridge University Press (2006). During 2002-2005 he was a sesquicentenary post-doctoral fellow in Work and Organisational

Studies at the University of Sydney. His current research focuses on aspects of the history of ideas and governance in late nineteenth and early twentieth century Australia. In 2014-2015 he was an Australian Prime Minister's Centre fellow, Museum of Australian Democracy, Old Parliament House Canberra.

Dr Nick Herd has a background in research, cultural policy and industry advocacy. He has worked in broadcasting at SBS Television and held senior posts with the Australian Broadcasting Tribunal, Australian Broadcasting Authority, Screen Producers Australia (as executive director), Screen Australia and the Australia Council. He is currently Head, Research and Policy at Ausfilm. He is the author of *Networking: Commercial Television in Australia* (2012), a history of commercial television.

Dr Carolyn Holbrook is a research fellow in the School of Social Sciences at Monash University. She is working with Professor James Walter on a history of public policy making in Australia. She is the author of *Anzac: The Unauthorised Biography*, (New South, 2014), which won the New South Wales Premiers' History Prize and the Queensland Premier's Literary Award in 2015. She has written articles on a range of subjects, including Australian soldier literature of the Great War, Labor Party immigration policy prior to 1947, the post-war reconstruction period in Australia and the Australian federation.

Dr Jodi McAlister is a lecturer in English at the University of Tasmania. Her PhD examined the history of representations of virginity loss and love in popular literatures. Her primary research interests are the history of love, sex, and popular texts. She is also a writer of fiction, and her debut novel *Valentine* will be published by

Penguin in 2017. She will definitely be recapping *Bachie* for many years to come.

Dr Clare Monagle is a Senior Lecturer in Modern History at Macquarie University. Usually, she works on the intellectual history of the Middle Ages. In 2012 she received an ARC DECRA to research the role of gender in medieval theology, and is currently working on a monograph tentatively titled *Sexing Scholasticism*. More broadly, Clare is interested in the history of discourses of purity, and how they pertain to to ideas of femininity. It is within this frame that she came to be interested in the role of food on Australian television.

David Nichols is a lecturer in urban planning at the Melbourne School of Design, University of Melbourne, specialising in urban and planning history. He has been a sporadic *Neighbours* viewer since the first episode, gaining knowledge put to good use during the 1980s–90s when he worked in children's magazines. At time of writing he is co-editing a book on cultural sustainability in country towns.

Dr Sarah Pinto is a historian who lectures in Australian Studies at Deakin University. Her research interests include public and popular history, the history and politics of emotions, gender and sexuality, and place and landscape. She is currently researching the commemoration of Indigenous peoples and histories in Australia's capital cities.

Dr David Rolph is an Associate Professor at the Faculty of Law, University of Sydney. He is one of Australia's leading media law academics, specialising in defamation and privacy law. He is the author of several books, including *Reputation, Celebrity and Defamation Law* (2008) and *Defamation Law* (2016), as well as numerous book chapters and journal articles. From 2007 to 2013, Dr Rolph was the editor of the *Sydney Law Review*, one of Australia's leading law journals. The research in this chapter was funded under the Australian Research Council's Discovery Projects funding scheme (project number DP120103538).

Dr Zora Simic is a Lecturer in History and Convenor of Women's and Gender Studies in the School of Humanities and Languages at the University of New South Wales. She has published widely on the past and present of Australian feminism, including her book *The Great Feminist Denial* (2008) co-authored with Monica Dux and has also written several articles on Sydney's western suburbs, including one focussed on the documentary series *Plumpton Babies* (2003) which like *Struggle Street* was filmed in the Mount Druitt area.